Tech Tides

Tech Tides

How Innovation Shapes Global Power

Edoardo Giglio

BLOOMSBURY
NEW YORK · LONDON · OXFORD · NEW DELHI · SYDNEY

BLOOMSBURY ACADEMIC
Bloomsbury Publishing Inc, 1385 Broadway, New York, NY 10018, USA
Bloomsbury Publishing Plc, 50 Bedford Square, London, WC1B 3DP, UK
Bloomsbury Publishing Ireland, 29 Earlsfort Terrace, Dublin 2, D02 AY28, Ireland

BLOOMSBURY, BLOOMSBURY ACADEMIC and the Diana logo are trademarks of
Bloomsbury Publishing Plc

First published in the United States of America 2025

Copyright © Bloomsbury Publishing Inc 2025

All rights reserved. No part of this publication may be: i) reproduced or transmitted in any form, electronic or mechanical, including photocopying, recording or by means of any information storage or retrieval system without prior permission in writing from the publishers; or ii) used or reproduced in any way for the training, development or operation of artificial intelligence (AI) technologies, including generative AI technologies. The rights holders expressly reserve this publication from the text and data mining exception as per Article 4(3) of the Digital Single Market Directive (EU) 2019/790.

Bloomsbury Publishing Inc does not have any control over, or responsibility for, any third-party websites referred to or in this book. All internet addresses given in this book were correct at the time of going to press. The author and publisher regret any inconvenience caused if addresses have changed or sites have ceased to exist, but can accept no responsibility for any such changes.

A catalog record for this book is available from the Library of Congress

ISBN: HB: 978-1-5381-9876-6
ePDF: 979-8-7651-5094-8
eBook: 978-1-5381-9877-3

Typeset by Sue Murray
Printed and bound in the United States of America

For product safety related questions contact productsafety@bloomsbury.com.

To find out more about our authors and books visit www.bloomsbury.com and sign up for our newsletters.

Contents

Introduction: Reviving the Corpse vii

PART ONE: THE INVENTION OF INNOVATION ECOSYSTEMS 1

Chapter 1: Israel: Choosing Innovation 3

Chapter 2: Taiwan: How to Become Invaluable 15

Chapter 3: Russia and Ukraine: Rethinking Innovation and Nations 25

PART TWO: THE DANGERS OF BEING OUTSIDE THE GLOBAL INNOVATION ECOSYSTEM 39

Chapter 4: North Korea: Outside by Choice 41

Chapter 5: Iran: Expelled 53

Chapter 6: Nigeria, Ethiopia, and South Africa: Struggling to Not Be a Have-Not 59

PART THREE: THE BENEFITS AND FEARS OF BEING INSIDE 71

Chapter 7: The United States, China, and India: Moonshots 73

Chapter 8: The World Brain: What Artificial Intelligence Is and Isn't 83

Chapter 9: Qatar, the United Arab Emirates, and Saudi Arabia: Leading the World in Sustainability 93

Chapter 10: Singapore: The Most Precious Passport 103

Chapter 11: The Human Factor: Digital Alchemy 107

Appendix A: Global Innovation Index, 2023	115
Appendix B: Global Artificial Intelligence	121
Appendix C: Global Trends, 2040	125
Index	127
About the Author	137

Introduction

Reviving the Corpse

The future geopolitical landscape won't be decided by tanks or planes, but rather by bytes and partnerships. In order to compete, we must future-proof countries—as well as individuals and companies—against becoming obsolete.

That's why, over my decades of work with governments, international organizations, philanthropies, corporations, universities, leading tech thinkers, and developers, I have constantly argued for the need to develop an "innovation ecosystem." These dynamic, synergistic communities can inspire the unimaginable by creating jobs, building economies, shaping exports and imports, and even curing disease and brokering peace.

Data is now more important than bullets for intelligence, whether it's market conditions, trends, or real-time military activity (more often seen by the general public as social media posts and propaganda). Those who prove faster and more agile will survive; merely look at Google, Amazon, and Wall Street to see who handles data exceptionally well and how information equates to profits in dollars. Only with a healthy innovation strategy in place can countries make themselves indispensable to the world, stave off invasion and manipulation by others, and keep themselves from falling behind.

What is a healthy innovation ecosystem? Consider Silicon Valley, where universities provide research and talent and where start-ups spark new ideas. Massive disruptions of entire business sectors are ever in the works, with companies taking the risk to create; active investors demanding more for their money; and local, state, and federal governments offering grants and effective tax and immigration policies, as well as protections that foster this unique environs. As you will learn, entire countries have devoted themselves to creating and growing their own unique innovation ecosystems, with some of the most important presently underway in the least likely of places. Interestingly, many of the major players in Silicon Valley aren't exclusively in Northern California, as emerging innovation ecosystems draw their attention and talent elsewhere, from far abroad. True innovation demands collaboration, and there's always the risk of resting on one's laurels while others are quietly leapfrogging over all you've accomplished.

In an oft-quoted speech to the Royal Academy, British Prime Minister Winston Churchill said, "Without tradition, art is a flock of sheep without a shepherd. Without innovation, it is a corpse." As the title of this introduction implores, we must revive the corpse. We all become stagnant, too proud and satisfied with our accomplishments, certainly distracted by our gadgets with too much information coming at us seemingly every second. Meanwhile, our enemies aren't so complacent or distracted, developing new tactics and innovations that will utterly overrun anyone in their path. Recent examples are the buildup to World War II and Hitler's rise, along with the current ascendance of China. Therefore, "the corpse" may be viewed as many things, including art, tradition, or culture. To me, the corpse is technology, military, health care, commercial and academic collaboration, sustainable development, and alternative power sources.

As an Italian who was adopted by Britain, I personally view Winston Churchill as the embodiment of stoicism and leadership in times of crisis. Before his rise to prime minister, Churchill was a young, pugnacious soldier who spanned eras. At only twenty-three years old, he was part of the last cavalry charge in British military history at the Battle of Omdurman, Sudan, and also served in Cuba, India, and South Africa, receiving several decorations for distinction. He then somehow managed to publish forty-three books (seventy-two volumes in total). Even if we ignore his leadership during France's "darkest" and England's "finest" hours of World War II, Churchill led a remarkable life. Then came World War II, with his voice of wisdom and mettle offering strength when it was most needed.

This book is about the myriad positive impacts of innovation, as well as the perils of falling behind. I begin with perhaps the most peculiar innovation ecosystem in the world, Israel, which had no choice but to invent its own form of collaboration between citizenry, government, commerce, and military in order to survive (see chapter 1). Ancient history begins in this part of the world and, ironically, the very future of innovation is presently being built in the Middle East (see chapter 9). When a country is part of the global innovation ecosystem, there is no limit to its potential. But when on the outside, intentionally like North Korea (see chapter 4) or purposely like Iran (see chapter 5), there is no end to the duplicity, domestic unrest, international hacking, theft, illegal arms trading, and overall danger for humanity.

We need only look at Russia's illegal invasion of Ukraine (see chapter 3) to realize what a lack of effective leadership and innovation has wrought.

Russia has suffered from lackluster research and development (R&D) investment since its glory days as a leader in space exploration, coupled with kickbacks to a select few oligarchs under authoritarian rule, to become a shadow of its former superpower self. Meanwhile, the mostly agrarian country of Ukraine has combined guerrilla and advanced strategies with new, mostly untested cutting-edge weapons to stymie the seemingly more advanced Russian military. Unsurprisingly, Ukrainian President Volodymyr Zelenskyy has welcomed comparisons to Winston Churchill, even invoking his words in a speech to the US Congress in December 2022: "Ukraine holds its lines and will never surrender."

In the West, the innovation challenge may be viewed as aging proprietary weapons systems that require ongoing maintenance, massive budget appropriations, and cumbersome design and development processes for any replacements. Retaining allies between changes in elected leadership is another challenge. The importance of the North Atlantic Treaty Organization (NATO) has come into question, as well as the very notion of nation-states, with the European Union being created, then undermined via Brexit. In the East, however, there's no debate or complacency, as China regularly launches entirely new navy fleets, all the while building roads and ports for trade with other nations, including a highly proprietary information technology network that spans entire regions. The latest world superpower is literally connecting new allies daily, expanding its military and strategic influence as needy nations welcome the inexpensive or free infrastructure with little concern for the actual costs, security vulnerabilities, and strings attached.

The world—old powers and tomorrow's leaders—must revive the corpse by sparking a new age of innovation, not solely for war but our survival as a species (see chapter 11). We are at the precipice of massive change via artificial intelligence and quantum computing, sustainable power sources, and cures for diseases that will forever alter humanity as we know it. Or we will have more haves and have-nots, war and compromise, strife instead of universally beneficial advancements for all.

This isn't just limited to the West or Far East, however: long-dormant nations are now rising and at last enjoying their moment of empowerment, especially in India and the Middle East. Other nations, most notably in Africa, are struggling to rebuild their former positions as leaders in trade and innovation, especially with young populations demanding improved education, job opportunities, and overall higher living standards (see chapter 6).

I am writing this introduction on September 1, 2023, exactly eighty-four years after Hitler invaded Poland. The leaders of France, Britain, and America were shocked that Germany would dare, defying diplomatic promises and naive appeasement. We are at another of those moments: It's midnight, the eve of catastrophe. Or, in my mind, we are on the verge of incredible advancements that will save millions of lives, give us a sustainable planet, and foster collaboration between innovators unseen in the history of humankind.

Soon the first quantum computers will be commercialized, an innovation full of promise and terror. Traditional computers would take centuries to perform the near-immediate calculations of a single quantum computer. Combined with emerging artificial intelligence, we will soon be able to make instant medical discoveries, curing both unique and chronic illnesses alike, while also encrypting our precious government, military, commercial, and personal data so that no foreign hacker can ever steal again and take advantage. Given such rapid advances, in artificial intelligence especially, we have no choice but to create guardrails: ethical development standards for AI tools and weapons that will soon not need humans at their controls. "The UN of AI" isn't that absurd to imagine (see chapter 8).

Digitization is so rapidly reshaping the geopolitical landscape that many nation-states are less powerful than corporations, with some smart countries using "digital ambassadors" to interact with technology leaders instead of government officials. The world is now experiencing hyperconnectivity, which will only increase.

When devising national strategies today, I focus my clients (governments, international organizations, corporations, philanthropies, and universities) on the five stages of innovation. By identifying where any nation or organization presently stands, I can then guide them toward their ultimate goals.

Five innovation strategies can future-proof against becoming obsolete:

1. Sustaining Innovation: Using conventional strategies (strategic roadmapping, R&D, acquisitions) to build new resources and skill sets.
2. Breakthrough Innovation: Forced exploration of unconventional skill domains and open innovation.
3. Disruptive Innovation: Reinventing your business model to stay relevant and competitive.
4. Basic Research: Investment in research and technology to build a cutting-edge advantage.
5. Frugal Innovation: Improving existing innovations by reducing complexity and cost.

Included in each chapter of this book are thorough historical and contemporary case studies of different nations and their respective innovation strategies and present status. Presented through the personal lessons I've witnessed over my many decades on the front lines of security, cyber, and strategic risk, each chapter details successes and mistakes that anyone trying to have any future whatsoever in our new information age should be aware of.

Introduction

* * *

So who am I, and why should you read this book, and maybe learn from the experiences, successes, and mistakes of myself and others?

To start, I was born on a battleground: Piacenza, Italy, where the Roman Empire fought Hannibal of Carthage in the Battle of Trebia after he miraculously crossed the Alps in 218 BCE, realizing rather brutally that the invasion would be bloody and unceasing. Rivalta Castle stands at the spot where Roman legions first saw Hannibal's war elephants—a literal giant innovation in battle—and where many knights later met to join the First Crusade. Ernest Hemingway visited after World War I and thought the Val Trebbia valleys to be the most beautiful in the world. My great-uncle was the commander of partisans fighting the fascists and Nazis during World War II, so it's safe to say that conflict runs in my veins.

I was the first non-British EU national to serve as a UK law enforcement officer, specializing in proactive covert intelligence and criminal investigations. Yes, I'm an Italian who worked for Scotland Yard, and I conducted countless undercover operations, posing as a drug trafficker, purchasing fake art, and infiltrating gangs utilizing the very first ATM skimming machines. I even had a price put on my head after conducting a sixteen-month operation resulting in the complete takedown of a renowned crime family.

In between operations, I continued to serve in criminal investigation units. During the latter part of my career, I focused increasingly on "high-tech crime." Just to proudly show you my nerd side, my father bought me a Commodore 64 weeks after they came out (I was six years old and ecstatic). I have always loved technology, even taking various information security courses in between my law enforcement and intelligence "day job."

I finally became a naturalized UK citizen in 2008 and, at the same time, there was a rapid rise of private security contractors from the Iraq and Afghanistan campaigns. Based on my background, I was recruited to assist with the design of the cyber, crisis management, and physical risk management plan for one of Europe's largest oil and gas firms in Basra, Iraq, in addition to other "special projects" on behalf of other clients, including the US Department of Defense.

Following two years in the private military "corporate" world, I founded my own company, which grew to more than 150 full-time employees, providing "special project" services for governments, top corporations, Forbes 20 high-net-worth individuals, major media outlets, and some of the largest philanthropic organizations. Our services were mostly centered around the unique fusion of physical, cyber, and media intelligence services for risk mitigation in emerging and frontier markets. I have worked in forty-eight countries over three continents, and have found myself in the middle of some of the most important historical events of the past two decades.

I was in the Middle East during the Arab Spring, including in Benghazi and Misrata, Libya, during the heaviest fighting, then in Liberia during the Ebola pandemic, where communications systems didn't collapse during the crisis. Over these many years I have worked with a vast number of international organizations, including at least fourteen United Nations agencies (including the International Telecommunication Union and the United Nations Children's Fund) as well as the World Health Organization and a plethora of nongovernmental organizations and government agencies.

I bring a unique mix of technology, operational, and on-the-ground expertise, and have also been at the intersection of tactics and strategies, both private and public. My experience is extremely rare, and I am proud to be associated with so many fine people around the world. In my field one must be constantly learning new strategies and technologies, so my education has been ongoing, whether at major universities or hands-on in the field. The outbreak of COVID-19 only added to my experience. I now lead a cyber and strategic risk government and public sector team, where I advise governments in the Middle East, Africa, and Asia on national strategies.

I know innovation and its players (posers, too), global trends, and maybe our future. Whether that future is bleak or bright is up to us. I know war and chaos, yet I remain optimistic.

This book is your tool for empowerment and change. Full of case studies and lessons learned, I hope you use it to fully grasp your present status on the five stages of innovation. Only then can you prepare for where you need to be tomorrow. I speak with great urgency.

I lost my father to brain cancer of the worst kind: multiple glioblastomas. More than two hundred thousand people worldwide die of this terrible disease each year, which is fatal within six months and has a survival rate of barely 7 percent. My father was too young, in his fifties, with so much more to give, and gone too soon. I'd give anything to have him back. I also now know that I share the genetic profile to suffer his same fate. This is why my work is so personal and urgent. Many of the innovations that are laid out in this book mean my own survival.

Together, we must revive the corpse, or become one.

Part I

THE INVENTION OF INNOVATION ECOSYSTEMS

1

Israel

Choosing Innovation

During a business trip to Israel a decade ago, providing security for a client, I found myself standing atop Masada, an ancient fortress as well as a symbol of Jewish defiance and heroism. The stillness of the Judaean Desert around me stood in stark contrast to the tumultuous history of the land beneath my feet. As the sun began to rise, the old tales of zealots and Roman legions echoed in my mind. However, it was the more recent history of this nation that truly captivated me.

Over breakfast in Tel Aviv, an elderly gentleman shared tales from his youth of scrambling for cover during air raids and the unparalleled spirit of this nascent nation. His stories were filled with moments of raw vulnerability and astounding resilience. With the desert winds carrying whispers of past trials, it became evident that Israel's story was about more than just survival. Israel flourishes against all odds.

Any new nation faces challenges. Whether liberated from a former colonizer, created when a major power suddenly breaks apart, or the product of a civil war divorce, borders are redrawn and all must embark on a new era alone. Israel is perhaps the most controversial country to appear in the twentieth century. Born from war, immediately invaded, ever threatened, no other nation has survived while surrounded by so many enemies. Still, Israel has thrived by inventing a most peculiar ecosystem for innovation, and has employed all five innovation strategies: frugal, basic research, disruptive, breakthrough, and sustaining.

Functionally, Israel's fusion of military, government, private business, citizenry, and allies is so symbiotic that it seems almost incestuous to outsiders. It's also genius, in that this small nation even exists, and is now a world leader in both military acumen and technology exports. Herein lies a case study that might not be copied by any other nation on Earth but includes different levels of innovation that must be understood, even if they aren't justifiable to most. Israel simply had no choice but to embrace such a unique ecosystem in its earliest days, which makes its present status more remarkable.

On May 14, 1948, the State of Israel declared its independence from British rule, as the territory, including long-held Palestinian lands, had been partitioned before and after World War II. Thousands of years in the making, the "lost tribes" scattered across the globe were finally coming home after the Second World War. The euphoria of the new nation also meant massive losses for Palestinians, as their own lands were divided by a United Nations (UN) mandate, only adding to the ire toward the Zionist state in a mostly Islamic region.

It's safe to say that Israel knew it was going to be attacked on its Independence Day. In fact, its leaders had been preparing for war for years prior to its official existence. Despite mandates that Israel could not have a defense industry, clandestine military manufacturing of bullets and basic weapons were created in earnest and were so secretive that one operation was located beneath a laundry. The Israel Defense Forces (IDF or "Tzahal") would quickly move from informal, strategic planning to the realities of the battlefield.

The First Arab–Israeli War erupted the next day, with Egypt, Syria, Jordan, and forces from Iraq attacking Israel. The war lasted ten months, but the new nation fought hard, and its planning saved lives and paid dividends, even winning territory beyond its original UN-mandated lands. Over seven hundred thousand Palestinians fled or were expelled, creating a massive refugee problem in the West Bank as well as in Jordan. Meanwhile, Israel had survived its first great threat.

An inventory of Israel at that moment is surreal: Israel's total population was 806,000, half that of Palestinian Arabs, and hardly 3 percent of the forty million people in neighboring enemy Arab states. It had a mere eighty-eight thousand soldiers to defend against millions of well-armed invaders on its borders. Israel had no natural resources, no exports, and no industry. Its nonsecular, parliamentary government was in its infancy, with mandatory rationing of food and oil, not to mention spiraling national debt. All of Europe was rebuilding after World War II and in no position to finance the building of another country. Upon its founding, Israel was a besieged and poor nation on the verge of either collapse or overthrow. US intelligence offered a very grim assessment of Israel, reporting: "Unless they are able to obtain significant outside aid . . . the Jews will be able to hold out no longer than two years."

Frugal innovation was of the utmost importance. Israel had to be both strict and creative. Israeli leaders quickly identified the country's strengths and weaknesses. And the weaknesses were many: In 1948, Israel only had one gun for every three soldiers, and virtually no heavy artillery or armored vehicles. There was no budget for defense spending and its allies were reluctant to fully support a nation teetering on the brink of failure.

Israel's strengths were, and remain, its people. During World War II the British had trained hundreds of Jews, who were now experienced in combat. They would train their fellow countrymen (and women) to defend the new nation. Independent and thus highly adaptable militias were born, mostly financed by locals or foreigners, so any notion of a command structure was problematic. Still, they fought.

Military conscription became central to Israel's national defense: Every eighteen-year-old Israeli would serve in the military (men served three years and women two years) and was expected to learn weapons, combat, defense, first aid, and strategy. Foreigners were welcome to enlist, as were Jews from abroad. Israeli Arabs, religious women, married individuals, and those deemed unfit were exempt. Any pacifists had to appear before a commission to state why they wouldn't serve their nation. "You must serve to become a citizen" was the mantra, and welcoming foreigners to enlist became a unique strength. Jews from abroad volunteered for training to protect the State of Israel, thus encouraging increased immigration, bringing new talents and skills to the young nation.

Knowing it was outnumbered by its neighboring enemies sixty-seven to one, Israel depended on muscle and frugal innovation to survive. More remote settlements were identified as the most vulnerable to invasion, so primitive ditches were dug and obstacles built to slow any enemy's approach. Later, Israel would retrofit a remote-controlled "toy" plane, bought for $850 in the United States, and use it for surveillance of its borders. This kept expensive jets on the ground and became the first functional use of "drones" in the world. By adapting conventional products for its uses, Israel has been ingenious in utilizing creativity to advance new technologies. This is the very definition of frugal innovation, and no country has done it better than Israel.

Reality also became the calling cry: Retreat wasn't possible because the people of Israel simply had nowhere else to go. Communications lines were critical; when modern phone lines were cut or destroyed, runners on foot spread updates between villages and leaders. Finally, faced with multiple enemies planning to invade at the same moment, Israeli leaders identified their enemies' greatest weakness: self-interest.

During the First Arab–Israeli War (1948), Egypt, Syria, Jordan, and Iraqi forces had their own targets and objectives in mind. Though the invaders were superior in number, Israel turned their assorted self-interests against them because they were never fully unified. Had they been, we would not be speaking of Israel today. Moreover, Israel did not abandon its remote villages and outposts, purposely slowing and frustrating the invasion, an "artificial strategic space" that limited casualties and cut enemy supply lines.

This was David versus Goliath. Instead of a sling and stone, Israel used trenches, human sweat, ancient communication systems, and the will of its people to defend itself, ultimately advancing and winning more territory. It's no wonder that Israel's strategy during the First Arab–Israeli War, including subsequent invasions by its neighbors, is now taught at military schools worldwide.

Diplomacy moved to the forefront after Israel proved that it could survive and exist on its own. When many of the Palestinian refugees settled in Jordan, Israel began courting King Abdullah of Jordan, who was friendly with former colonizer Britain, to discuss a Palestinian state, showing a shared concern for the refugees and the need for peace. It worked, and Israel soon turned its enemy into a partner.

Reparations negotiated with Germany for Holocaust victims and refugees, totaling $1.5 billion in US dollars in 1953 (or $3,000 USD for each of the half-million Jews resettled in Israel), underwrote the young country's development. Foreign investment from Jewish people worldwide also helped, and has since become a critical source of support for Israel. Dams, roads, and other infrastructure projects flourished across Israel in the 1950s, employing the populace and bolstering its defenses. Over one million Jewish immigrants were welcomed into Israel as well, swelling its population and military readiness, while also bringing new talents and skills. Yet the country's economy languished. Early foreign trade attempts by Israeli ambassadors included a trip to sell oranges and other fruit to South America, where those products were already plentiful. There were few new trade deals and the emerging nation struggled with any trade whatsoever, its economy mostly financed by sympathetic foreigners, with enemies still at Israel's borders.

At this moment, Israel's unique hybridization of business, government, civilians, and military emerged. Thanks to mandatory conscription, all Israelis shared a stake in the national defense, but an actual economy needed to be a priority. The Pamaz Agreement in the 1950s changed the game, allowing direct subsidies from the government to Israeli companies, especially those that exported products. Its currency was changed from the Palestinian pound (on par with British sterling) to the Israeli lira, which made fluctuations in foreign currency exchanges problematic and unpredictable. Israeli companies were encouraged to place their proceeds from foreign trade into foreign accounts. This may seem like common sense in today's age of multinational megacorporations, but the Pamaz Agreement sped exports while also making allies of foreign countries that held and exchanged Israel's trade accounts, giving them a true financial stake in their shared success and future.

Despite millions of dollars in donations to Israel from Americans (mostly Jews, but a growing number of Christians supporting the "Second Coming" and holy Jerusalem), the US government remained hesitant to fully back Israel, financially or internationally. America offered modest aid while also maintaining ties and influence with oil-producing Arab states, which decried punishment for the crimes of World War II. The Cold War changed that, most critically for the economic and technological direction of Israel.

In July 1956, Egypt nationalized the Suez Canal, which allowed two-thirds of Europe's oil transit. Backed by the Union of Soviet Socialist Republics (USSR), Egypt was defiant. Then, on October 29, the Israeli military invaded Egypt and, backed by French and British troops, advanced to within ten miles of the canal. The world was on edge, and the USSR almost entered the conflict, putting the United States in a tenuous position. Fearing this regional battle could become another world war, the United States eventually demurred, letting Egypt (and the USSR) appear victorious. Now Israel was seen as an aggressor in the region, and France and Britain had blanched their essential relations with the United States.

Hostilities escalated, yet Israel continued to plan and innovate. From frugal to basic research, then to disruptive innovation—"moonshot" programs included—Israeli leaders and engineers rapidly advanced its military.

For example, most of Israel's air force was supplied by France. The Mirage IIICJ fighter jet was cutting-edge, the first Mach 2 plane in Israel's arsenal, but it needed to meet the nation's unique needs. The Mirage was a relatively short-range aircraft, which Israeli engineers fixed by stripping out advanced avionics equipment to increase fuel-carrying capacity while also reducing maintenance costs. The Mirage's two 20 millimeter (mm) caliber cannons were also determined inadequate, so Israel defied standard aircraft designs to equip its fighter jets with two or four 30 mm cannons, bringing devastating power and destruction to both the air and ground.

Israel no longer needed foreign troops, only foreign weapons to adapt, as conscription and immigration had built a well-trained, well-armed Israeli military numbering 240,000. This was enough for an effective defense, but too small to sustain a prolonged conflict. The emerging nation now had a customized and impressive military, a growing export economy, and was finally enjoying support from foreign allies—a step up from frugal innovation only a decade earlier. Even the United States privately offered emergency military aid to Israel, despite public promises to stay out of any conflict in the Middle East.

The powder keg exploded in June 1967. Chest-thumping by Syria and Egypt (and its USSR ally) had signaled another invasion was coming, and Israel was determined to strike first. At dawn on June 5, using strict radio silence, Israel launched 183 aircraft, bombing and decimating Egyptian aircraft and bases. The adapted Mirage fighter jets proved their worth; since they required less refueling, their larger cannons inflicted far more damage. Within the first three hours of the Six-Day War, Israel gained immediate air superiority: Egypt lost 293 of its 500 aircraft, while Israel lost only 19. The war was a rout: Syria lost two-thirds of its air force and Jordan was left militarily ineffective. Egypt and the USSR were embarrassed, and the region would never be the same.

Israel seized the Sinai Peninsula, Golan Heights, Gaza Strip, and the West Bank, including East Jerusalem, quadrupling its size in only six days. Today, diplomatic debates still rage over the territories seized in 1967. A new era was opened for Israel: one of military dominance in the region and weakened enemies. Most importantly, the world was assured that it could survive, maybe even thrive.

Israel did not rest on its laurels, as there is always too much at stake for the "Chosen People." When France placed an arms embargo on Israel in 1968, Israeli leaders decided it was time to "invent" their own fighter jet. Following its modus operandi of frugal, then disruptive (at times clandestine) innovation, Israel "acquired" the designs for France's next-generation Mirage fighter jets. Major modifications were made to the cockpit, landing gear, cooling systems, and fuel tanks, then Israel selected General Electric's J79 turbojet engine, revealing their homemade Nesher fighter jet in under two years. Regular modifications have led to the legendary Kfir fighter jets, first launched in 1975.

All of Israel participates in its national security, via conscription, and the country has an expansive military industry. Regional skirmishes were regular throughout the 1970s and 1980s, and rocket attacks from Palestinian neighborhoods were all too common. Manufacturing companies, especially those in technology, are therefore encouraged to be dual-purposed—meaning that their output can be quickly adapted for military use. Whether commercial or retail, heavy industry or a basic service, any Israeli entity must be easily mobilized for the national defense. This hybrid ecosystem, agile and experienced after decades of war, is essential to the survival of the state. This has never been more important, given the rise of the Palestinian Liberation Organization (PLO), Hamas, and Hezbollah, nonstate adversaries that further complicate Israel's reality. Guerrilla warfare is the norm, and enemy nations remain at its borders, so the Israeli government, military, industries, services, and citizenry must also acknowledge and defend against all state and nonstate adversaries.

Israel has been the leading producer of drones since 1980. What most consider a recent technology is actually over forty years old and has been led by Israel to maintain surveillance high above its borders. What started as a $850 toy airplane has become the vaunted Hermes and Heron drone systems, designed in tandem with the Israeli government, IDF, Elbit, and Israel Aerospace Industries. While actual numbers are difficult to report, due to national security (many of these systems are in use domestically) as well as foreign deals, Israel has exported at least $4.8 billion in drones since 2014, around 10 percent of its total military exports.

Given the effectiveness of drones on the battlefield, as well as potential markets worldwide, China has identified this segment as strategically important and is investing heavily to surpass Israel's drone leadership in both sales and technology. America's Boeing Corporation has already spent $300 million trying to match Israel's drone program, and recently invested at least another $450 million in start-ups focused on this technology. But Israel spent only $850 on a toy airplane, then changed the face of aerial warfare forever.

Today, this controversial country is a leader. No enemy nation dares invade Israel. Its "Iron Dome" air defense system (including automated guided missiles, radar, drones, and early warning systems) is the envy of the world. So is its cybertechnology: During the dot-com boom of the late 1990s, Tel Aviv was the Silicon Valley of the Middle East, boasting thousands of Internet start-ups. Today, tech start-ups in Israel outperform Silicon Valley and touch every sector: transportation, renewable power, education, health care, software development, artificial intelligence, sports betting and, of course, the military. Predictably, many of Israel's military veterans, soldiers, and technologists are now in the business sector, sharing their skills with new arrivals, further cementing the economy's dual-purpose ecosystem for innovation.

To fully grasp Israel's technological focus and future, look to the remote outpost of Negev and the sprawling "city in the desert," Beer Sheba. This 650-acre innovation hub grows daily, filled with tech companies, medical centers, government institutions, and universities all gathering to invent. American companies, including IBM, Dell, Amazon, Cisco, Microsoft, and Google, are on site as well to collaborate and recruit from the tens of thousands of Israelis, students, and immigrants who are advancing across the whole spectrum of cyber "verticals" that encompass R&D, project management, and integration.

In total, more than 250 global companies have research and development (R&D) labs in Israel. This is serious business. What many of these Fortune 500 companies and international investors view as Israel's most important asset hearkens back to its very founding seventy-five years ago: its people. Israel's openness to researchers and students worldwide has made it a stronger state. While the United States depends on M-1 and "genius" visas to attract foreign business and technical talent, Israel utilizes the skills of those who long to return to the "promised land" (either for faith or to help the nation survive) to grow and blossom. Interestingly, many people are moving to Israel not for religious reasons at all, but solely for the vast opportunities of its economy.

Such massive immigration has increased Israel's population from its original 806,000 in 1948 to nearly ten million in 2022. Critically, its birth rate is also higher than most developed countries and its neighbors, ensuring future generations of workers. This population explosion has led to decreased conscription terms (men now serve thirty-two months and women two years), with select exemptions for pacifists, Arabs, ultra-Orthodox Jews, and those unfit to serve.

Technology (drones, cameras, and sensors) now performs most of the surveillance of borders and remote regions, so a smaller standing military is needed. Elite military units (Mossad, Metsada, et al.) function independently, and it's rarely a shock when hostile states have their clandestine nuclear programs halted by Israel. Even today, Israel does not acknowledge that it has nuclear warheads, which highlights both its national secrecy and confidence.

Innovation remains a cornerstone for this one country. Unit 9900 of the IDF, a selective intelligence squad that monitors satellite and intelligence data, may be the most groundbreaking military operation ever, and recruits Israelis who would otherwise be exempt from military service. Those diagnosed with autism spectrum disorder often exhibit certain high-functioning capabilities that Unit 9900 fosters and encourages, such as incredibly detailed mapping, decoding, identifying cyberthreats, programming, and special operations. It also allows these "specially gifted soldiers" to be part of their nation's defense. It's far more than a job, and the fact that these unique soldiers aren't on government welfare (or considered a lost cause) is important for both them and the greater economy of Israel. This program has been so successful that the United Kingdom is now launching its own version of Unit 9900.

Other nations have had no choice but to take note and mimic Israel—its former enemies included. Israel's success has seen the thawing of hostilities between itself and Saudi Arabia, with whom relations have improved. Applying some of the same lessons learned in the creation of Israel's innovative ecosystem, Saudi Arabia's sprawling "NEOM" initiative in its Tabuk Province may be the pinnacle. This futuristic "special economic zone" will be an entirely new city and ecosystem, with Saudi Arabia attracting the leading minds in technology, education, economics, climate and, yes, defense, in a new form of collaborative innovation. NEOM offers hope for a more peaceful Middle East as well as major technological and societal breakthroughs, with Israel's inclusion a momentous message for the world.

Israel is by no means an Eden. It has survived, but still has no natural resources. The symbiosis of government, military, industry, and citizenry works well for Israelis, but there's always the Palestinian question, not to mention the lack of any two-state solution. The country's nonsecular parliamentary government has faced deep divisions, with prime ministers coming and going, then coming back again. Benjamin Netanyahu has returned to power in Israel, and is courting the far-right fringes while also diminishing the Supreme Court's power, inflaming tensions and sparking protests nationwide. Netanyahu has also been avoiding felony charges and a trial for bribery, which undermines his credibility domestically and internationally. The ultra-Orthodox Jewish population has become a powerful bloc, and the average Israeli may question why they must serve in the military when others don't. Every nation has its challenges, and Israel's pale in comparison to some, but its national stability must remain at the forefront as it matures as a country while still facing multiple enemies.

A surprise attack by Hamas on the morning of October 7, 2023—which saw over five thousand rockets launched and insurgents entering Israel from the Gaza Strip in the first hours—highlights the country's daily threats and unceasing conflict. With hundreds of Israeli hostages taken, thousands dead, and thousands more injured on both sides, Prime Minister Netanyahu declared "we are at war" and called up reservists. How a country so heavily surveilled was fully surprised by such an attack is still being debated, including questions about Israel's vaunted "Iron Dome" air defenses being overwhelmed by Hamas's rockets.

What is clear is that politics, distraction, and arrogance played parts. Israel had become too dependent on high-tech surveillance for its security, suffering from too much incoming data that is often difficult to decipher and put into rapid tactical strategy. While Netanyahu was busy catering to far-right allies and revamping Israeli leadership, Hamas was borrowing many of Israel's own frugal innovation methodologies in planning the attack. As in the First Arab–Israeli War, Hamas adopted only face-to-face communications, avoiding easily intercepted cell phone and online messaging, and used its muscle to build a vast tunnel system below Gaza. Drones and cyber and radar systems proved poor replacements for ancient creativity and sweat, making the attack shockingly effective. Israel's military dictum and equipment have overrun Gaza, creating a humanitarian and refugee crisis.

Once more, Jordan and Egypt are offering aid to uprooted Palestinians, just as Iran's fingerprints are being revealed on weapons and advanced rockets used in the attack. The United States has not wavered in its support for Israel, even as its own political polarization stymied a rapid response and funding. Critically, US intelligence admitted in November 2023 that it had lost focus on monitoring Hamas after the 9/11 attacks, including invasions of Afghanistan and Iraq. Like 9/11, Hamas's surprise invasion was also a failure of imagination. Motorized paragliders and basic armaments were utilized by Hamas, showing how the most frugal of innovations can have deadly effects. By not maintaining all five innovation strategies, depending too much on just one, Israel had lethal vulnerabilities that were fully exploited by Hamas. Meanwhile, the entire world watches nervously, hoping that this doesn't expand into a regional conflict, nonstate actors and proxies included.

This handling of the Gaza Strip and Palestinians signals a new phase in Israel's defensive posture. Anti-Semitism is spreading as sympathies for Palestinians living in the Gaza Strip grow, so Israel must balance its military response with international apprehension while ensuring its own innovation ecosystem isn't undermined after so much blood, sweat, tears, treasure, and ingeniousness over decades. Despite the recent thawing of relations with former enemies, Israel will remain the focus of the tinderbox that is the Middle East. The United Kingdom and Europe have NATO for protection; the United States has the Atlantic and Pacific oceans. Israel only has itself.

Israel, which began as a group of war-torn refugees on UN-mandated lands, is now a top-fifty exporter worldwide, jumping double digits year to year to almost $165 billion in 2022. Military, technology, diamonds, cotton, and even Israeli fruit are all finding eager markets abroad. Accounting for over one-third of its half-trillion-dollar national gross domestic product (GDP), exports are now essential for the survival of Israel. So too are allies, former enemies included.

There is true hope and promise in the Holy Land. Born from war, Israel is now a beacon of progress and prosperity. From the most frugal of innovation—while simultaneously surviving multiple invasions—to relying on basic research and disruptive technology to become a leader in drones and dual-purpose industries for both trade and defense, Israel's status as a breakthrough and sustaining leading innovator in multiple sectors is truly remarkable. This small nonsecular nation has fully evolved in seventy-five years.

Today, Israel is the most unique symbiotic ecosystem for development, innovation, and defense on Earth. Whether other countries can copy Israel's unique ecosystem is open to debate, but few question its will to survive.

BIBLIOGRAPHY

Anti-Defamation League. "Founding of the State of Israel, May 14, 1948." September 1, 2016. https://www.adl.org/resources/glossary-term/founding-state-israel-may-14-1948.

BBC News. "1967 War: Six Days That Changed the Middle East." June 5, 2017. https://www.bbc.com/news/world-middle-east-39960461.

BBC News. "Israel Supreme Court Showdown over Controversial Judicial Reform." September 12, 2023. https://www.bbc.com/news/world-middle-east-66751706.

Bridgwater, Adrian. "How Israel Became a Technology Startup Nation." *Forbes*, February 21, 2020. https://www.forbes.com/sites/adrianbridgwater/2020/02/21/how-israel-became-a-technology-startup-nation/?sh=22d673e6780e.

Egozi, Arie. "Israel Asks Industry to Develop New Long-Range, Stealthy Armed Drones." *Breaking Defense* (November 11, 2022). https://breakingdefense.com/2022/11/israel-asks-industry-to-develop-new-long-range-stealthy-armed-drones.

Federman, Josef, and Issam Adwan. "Hamas Surprise Attack Out of Gaza Stuns Israel and Leaves Hundreds Dead in Fighting, Retaliation." *AP News*, October 7, 2023. https://apnews.com/article/israel-palestinians-gaza-hamas-rockets-airstrikes-tel-aviv-11fb98655c256d54ecb5329284fc37d2.

Heller, Christian H. "Weakness into Strength: Overcoming Strategic Deficits in the 1948 Israeli War for Independence." *The Strategy Bridge*, September 24,

2018. https://thestrategybridge.org/the-bridge/2018/9/24/weakness-into-strength-overcoming-strategic-deficits-in-the-1948-israeli-war-for-independence.

History.com. "Suez Crisis." November 9, 2009. https://www.history.com/topics/cold-war/suez-crisis.

Israel Defense Forces. "Our Soldiers." https://www.idf.il/en/mini-sites/our-soldiers/.

Katz, Yaakov. "Why Israel Has the Most Technologically Advanced Military on Earth." *New York Post*, January 29, 2017. https://nypost.com/2017/01/29/why-israel-has-the-most-technologically-advanced-military-on-earth.

Kaur Rai, Selina. "What Were the Causes and Consequences of the 1948 Arab–Israeli War?" *E-International Relations*, January 15, 2014. https://www.e-ir.info/2014/01/15/what-were-the-causes-and-consequences-of-the-1948-arab-israeli-war-2.

Leone, Dario. "The Story of the IAF Skyhawk Pilot Who Shot Down Two Syrian MiG-17s Flying an A-4 Fitted with French-Designed and Israeli-Manufactured 30 mm DEFA Cannon." *The Aviation Geek Club*, May 13, 2023. https://theaviationgeekclub.com/the-story-of-the-iaf-skyhawk-pilot-who-shot-down-two-syrian-mig-17s-flying-an-a-4-fitted-with-french-designed-and-israeli-manufactured-30-mm-defa-cannon.

Lieber, Dov. "In Israel, Army Service Is Required for All. That Could Now Change." *Wall Street Journal*, May 12, 2023. https://www.wsj.com/articles/in-israel-army-service-is-required-for-all-that-could-now-change-2c76624d#.

Miller, Naomi. "Beer Sheba—Israel's Innovation Capital." *The Jewish News*, July 22, 2020. https://thejewishnews.com/2022/07/22/column-beer-sheba-israels-innovation-capital.

Peck, Michael. "How Israel's Air Force Won the Six-Day War in Six Hours." *National Interest*, June 2, 2017. https://nationalinterest.org/blog/the-buzz/how-israels-air-force-won-the-six-day-war-six-hours-20980.

Pomfret, Richard. "Export Policies and Performance in Israel." Kiel Working Paper no. 27, Kiel Institute of World Economics, January 1975. https://www.econstor.eu/bitstream/10419/47253/1/238489493.pdf.

Rubin, Shira. "The Israeli Army Unit That Recruits Teens with Autism." *The Atlantic*, January 6, 2016. https://www.theatlantic.com/health/archive/2016/01/israeli-army-autism/422850/.

Solomon, Shoshanna. "From 1950s Rationing to Modern High-Tech Boom: Israel's Economic Success Story." *Times of Israel*, April 18, 2018. https://www.timesofisrael.com/from-1950s-rationing-to-21st-century-high-tech-boom-an-economic-success-story.

World Bank. "World Development Indicators." https://datatopics.worldbank.org/world-development-indicators.

Yager, Avi. "The Transformation of the Israel Defense Forces Avi Jager International Institute for Counter-Terrorism." *Naval War College Review*, Spring 2021. https://digital-commons.usnwc.edu/cgi/viewcontent.cgi?article=8185&context=nwc-review.

Yin, David. "Secrets to Israel's Innovative Edge." *Forbes*, June 5 2016. https://www.forbes.com/sites/davidyin/2016/06/05/secrets-to-israels-innovative-edge/?sh=190673534aec.

2

Taiwan

How to Become Invaluable

Let's start this chapter with a thought exercise: Pick a country. Now consider all its contributions to the world, its innovations and influence, and its products and people. Next, tally this single nation's impact on all of humanity. This may be humbling, depending on which country you chose, but it's an important inventory of an entire nation's tangible value to the world.

Now render that nation moot, utterly erased from memory, along with all of its contributions to the larger world. Will the disruption be small or seismic? Will the rest of the world stop, all of humanity suddenly incapable of functioning? Or are there other countries that offer comparable products and people, innovations and influence, that will make the absence of one country's offerings easier to accept?

If Canada disappears, surely European hockey and American maple syrup will fill the void. Australia could create a fine film industry and gladly welcome more tourism if, say, New Zealand was suddenly struck from history. The very concept of some countries gives them more weight than they presently hold—Greece's "great experiment" with democracy millennia ago, or the aura of mystery surrounding the Asian steppes, from whence a great Mongol horde and the Huns emerged to terrify the known world. Today, though, at this very instant, what country is irreplaceable to everyone?

The answer is easy. And it's tiny.

Geographically, it is half the size of Scotland and slightly bigger than the state of Maryland. It's an island nation somewhat protected by natural barriers, yet vulnerable to neighboring nations with long histories of invasion and conquest. It has no military presence. Untouchable, no, but its advanced products made by its highly trained people are so critical that all the world's superpowers claim the right to defend or invade it at any time.

Taiwan.

At the mere mention of this small island nation, one immediately thinks of technology: clean rooms fabricating advanced microchips; a highly educated populace so efficient that they are more notion than actual individuals. Taiwan is irreplaceable because it is synonymous with semiconductors, a status that lends it a "silicon shield" of protection. It's the perfect defense because other nations simply couldn't function without Taiwan's exports.

I clearly remember walking through the bustling streets of Taipei many years ago, feeling the pulsating energy of a nation on the cusp of something monumental. An elderly vendor, noticing my curiosity, handed me a strange souvenir: a silicon wafer. Little did I know that this seemingly inconspicuous item would come to symbolize the world's reliance on this single island nation, tiny yet formidable. It's easy to marvel at towering giants, the superpowers of our world, but sometimes, true strength is found in the least suspected and most overlooked places. "Be invaluable" is not just a mantra, but a lesson I've taken from the heart of Taiwan. It's a message that I stress with all my clients, big and small, to focus on something that makes them less vulnerable and far more critical in the global ecosystem.

This one nation's microscopic yet advanced silicon wafers, made mostly by the eponymous Taiwan Semiconductor Manufacturing Company (TSMC), have made it invaluable. Taiwan dominates the world's semiconductor industry, owning around 60 percent of the global market and earning over $175 billion USD in 2022, growing by double digits for the seventh consecutive year. While other microchip manufacturers have been suffering from less demand and lower profits, Taiwan is booming.

It wasn't always this way, but the current situation is very much by design. This is the story of one country outsourcing a critically important product—in hindsight, surrendering its very future—as another took a great gamble and defied all of the experts to seize an entire industry.

Throughout history, Taiwan has seemingly belonged to everyone else: the Dutch, Spanish, Chinese, Japanese, and then the Chinese again. After a brief period of democracy, Taiwan now has the paradoxical existence of being independent yet claimed by China once more.

Taiwan's emergence as the dominant semiconductor provider began in the early 1970s, with the help of the United States and at US expense. Using basic research and disruptive, breakthrough innovation strategies, Taiwan wisely grabbed an emerging technology, then invested in its people to become the global leader.

The Radio Corporation of America (RCA) was started by General Electric in 1917 and had been a pioneer in early transistors. By 1970, as the company sought more military applications for its products, the government of Taiwan was launching a total reengineering of its own economy, with America's guidance. Mass migration of Chinese nationals forced land reforms, a full retooling of Taiwan's defunct currency, and a total refocusing on education—a change from its agrarian past. Unlike other Asian nations that utilized import-dependent policies while rebuilding after a world war, Taiwan dreamed big of being an exporter.

RCA and Taiwan would work together closely to invent the semiconductor industry while actively outsourcing American production to this eager upstart. Taiwan underwrote the travel and training costs for dozens of young engineers to live and work in the United States, learning RCA's products and processes, and the $10 million spent on this foreign foray resulted in the largest return on investment in human history. Industrial Technology Research Institute (ITRI), formed in 1973, signed a technology transfer licensing agreement with RCA in 1976, and the first three-inch wafer fabrication plant was opened in 1977. The rest is history, literally. RCA was defunct by 1987 and Taiwan owns the global semiconductor industry today.

The United States is now paying a steep price to get this industry back. In 2022, the US government's CHIPS and Science Act allocated $52.7 billion to encourage domestic microchip development and production. TSMC obliged, initially promising $12 billion (now $40 billion total) to build an advanced fabrication plant outside of Phoenix, Arizona. Just consider the historical price tag: $10 million spent by Taiwan in the 1970s is worth over $90 billion today!

But this isn't the 1970s. Is the United States even making the right investment? Will this be "old" chip technology or the new, cutting-edge semiconductors that brought us 5G (soon 6G) innovations for much faster wireless speeds? Education and training are also major hurdles to bringing TSMC's new Arizona plant online, as estimated construction costs are spiraling to ten times higher in the United States than in Taiwan. Then there are the cultural differences between any two countries when attempting a new, foreign operation.

Overshadowing TSMC's venture are worries about national security. Not included in Taiwan's dominant semiconductor industry market share is another category: military and classified intelligence systems requiring secret semiconductor designs that few are allowed to know about. While an American corporation once gladly cooperated in outsourcing production to an eager foreign nation, Taiwan and TSMC leaders are rightly concerned about granting access to vital commercial and military semiconductor production designs. Taiwan knows the value of its "silicon shield."

With so much at stake, and the entire world dependent on Taiwan's exports, a candid study of the two countries vying to control this tiny island nation is in order. China and the United States are the undisputed world superpowers, yet their innovation strategies are as far apart as their governments.

No nation on Earth has benefited more from other nations' outsourcing than China. Home to nearly 30 percent of the total manufacturing output worldwide, China's costs are 50 to 80 percent lower than those of developed nations. Outsourced services have also become a $175 billion industry for China, targeting international medical and financial markets. China has designed entire cities populated to serve the needs of foreign companies: Apple products are built at the massive "city within a city" Foxconn plant in Zhengzhou, which employs around three hundred thousand workers, while the Dongguan YueYuen shoe factory in the Guangdong Province employs up to fifty thousand workers to make shoes for premier brands, including Nike, Adidas, Reebok, and New Balance. China boasts massive modern-day economic development, with a miraculous GDP growth of nearly 10 percent for decades that has raised the incomes and living standards of hundreds of millions of people. Yet it has overlooked one critical lesson.

It isn't invaluable.

Government-mandated lockdowns to prevent the spread of COVID-19 (and its variants) revealed a major weakness in China's "outsource here" economy. The country's GDP promptly dropped to 3 percent in 2022. Foreign companies struggled with supply chain issues due to a lack of Chinese workers providing inexpensive products, and rare protests by the Chinese people against their government's zero-COVID stance have revealed domestic unrest previously unseen beyond the country's borders. China simply cannot afford to have a billion Chinese people underemployed and idle.

Perhaps more troubling are the reactions of business leaders who simply won't tolerate supply chain disruptions for long. The production and hundreds of thousands of jobs at Foxconn in Zhengzhou are now seen by Apple as a corporate weakness, and the corporation is making plans for factories in Vietnam and elsewhere. Vietnam is also being eyed by Nike and other footwear giants, not just due to the zero-COVID disruptions in China but to repair corporate images of young and impoverished Chinese workers assembling expensive sneakers for wealthy foreign consumers. The lowest manufacturing costs will remain a focus among major international companies, so India and other nations are aggressively courting companies eager to employ their people through outsourced labor.

Though China is losing major foreign employers and investment, what it has accomplished during its rapid rise can't be ignored. The Chinese Belt and Road Initiative brought much-needed development to Africa, eastern Europe, southeast Asia, and even South America. By mixing huge infrastructure projects (overland roads as well as sea routes) with major technological upgrades across 150 countries, China is investing in mostly ignored regions to spur serious economic development. This has created new commerce, cut trade costs, and generated much goodwill toward China.

New roads and technology come with many strings attached for the nations that stand to benefit. This is most obvious in China's parallel initiative, known as the Digital Silk Road. Many confuse the Belt and Road Initiative with the Digital Silk Road one, as both are financed and led by China. New roads and sea routes for faster, cheaper trade are far easier to grasp than the breadth of a comprehensive digital infrastructure network. Chinese tech firms such as Huawei are integrating across these networks, triggering fears of digital spying, insecure financial transactions, and the constant concern of hindered innovation. Government-subsidized, and thus cheaper for the end consumer, Huawei and other Chinese technology "partners" in the Digital Silk Road seem to offer an amazing deal—"free" or less expensive digital infrastructure—but the long-term costs are already becoming clear.

The notion of franchises is often used to explain the concept of entire countries taking advantage of China's digital "gifts." Yet any franchise can be cut off by headquarters (i.e., China) when its rigid rules aren't followed. Indeed, a "techno-authoritarian" top-down deployment has become pervasive, while the growing influence of Chinese companies trying to manage and rewrite global e-commerce and technology standards, as well as monitor and exploit social media, is already being felt. However effective in the long term, China is continuing to spend [tens of billions **AU: in USD, or yuan? Please clarify/rewrite.**] each year, even as its own economy is struggling, while recipient countries become so dependent that there seems to be no escape.

Such bold and ambitious initiatives have made China the sole threat to American worldwide dominance. Militarily, China has twice as many active service members in its military as the United States (2.8 million versus 1.4 million), and a navy with more total ships (355 versus 296). Its manufacturing power is on full display, as China launches new warships regularly, while the complex budgeting, design, testing, and deployment of new armaments by the United States can take decades.

In 2023, the United States will officially have spent over $800 billion on defense. But that's only a number on paper. It doesn't include surveillance, intelligence and special operations, or contractors and support for allies (Ukraine being the biggest and latest example of rapid military appropriations). Actual US military spending is well over a trillion dollars per year.

Exactly what is the United States defending itself against? During the Cold War it was the USSR; now Russia, a dictatorship dependent on oil exports that has been stymied while again invading its agrarian neighbor, Ukraine. Other than nuclear intercontinental ballistic missiles (ICBMs), the United States was hardly vulnerable to its sole "superpower" competitor. In 2023, Russia doubled its defense budget to $100 billion USD (one-tenth of the US budget) due to the plummeting value of the ruble after its invasion of Ukraine. China will spend less than $300 billion on defense in 2023. To defend its 330 million citizens, the United States spends around $2,500 on the military per citizen, while China spends around $190 per citizen. The United States alone is responsible for approximately 40 percent of total global military spending;

it spends more on defense than 144 countries combined. Understanding this, Americans should be nervous: without our decades of bloated spending and aged systems that need ongoing and expensive maintenance, foreign competitors are capable of building entirely new navies and supplying far more armies with the most advanced weapons. Surely, the United States needs to budget far more to defend itself from its own military spending!

The worst example of American military bureaucracy is the F-35 fighter jet, known as the most expensive weapon in human history. Imagined in 2001, and designed for production by 2006, this single-seat stealth jet uses a futuristic helmet that lets pilots control every instrument. Yet it has been plagued with issues from the start, including problems with its stealth paint, pilots who become confused by too much incoming data, and general engine and flight failures, including vibrations. Eerily enough, it even has a higher rate of being struck by lightning than other jets! Initially, an entire squadron of F-35s for all branches of the American military was sold for the "low" price of $233 billion. It has since cost $1.6 trillion. The original designs were still not in full production by 2016. Even worse, the per-flight-hour cost for the F-35 is double the cost of other fighter jets already in the arena. Modified versions of the F-35, such as Lockheed Martin's ironically named F-35A Lightning II, are slowly being rolled out to replace the US Air Force's time-tested F-16s, while others are still grounded due to recurring problems.

Obviously, the best new technology built with the biggest budgets doesn't equate to actual strength. Today, the harsh realities of the United States' former "sole threat," Russia, have brought the myths of military might to light. Russia's invasion of Ukraine has been a disaster, its aged equipment and poorly trained soldiers stymied at every turn by Ukrainian civilians defending their homeland. Meanwhile, China is watching these developments closely, as both an ally to Russia and possible opponent to the United States.

Yet Taiwan remains China's focus. Under the "One China" principle, the entire South China Sea and the island of Taiwan must be under the control of mainland China. Meanwhile, Taiwan is defiant, entrenched in the belief that it was never under modern Chinese control, which dates from over a century ago to today. Global economics and diplomacy further shape this debate, straining global relations. For example, only thirteen countries presently recognize Taiwan as a sovereign nation; the United States does, but the United Kingdom does not.

The small island nation with a "silicon shield" now has the attention of the world.

In April 2023, China held "defensive maneuvers" that included a full invasion scenario as well as sealing off Taiwan from the rest of the world. Meanwhile, the United States urged calm and advised restraint by China, even as Taiwan's government held a mass celebration of its freedom.

Then, in May 2023, former US national security advisor Robert O'Brien remarked that the United States and its allies "are never going to let those factories fall into Chinese hands." While these were fiery comments by a former official from a former administration, consider the implications: The United States would rather destroy Taiwan's semiconductor factories than allow China to control them. This means that 60 percent of the world's semiconductor market (consumer and "other") presently produced by Taiwan would disappear. Such draconian talk ignores other factors: exactly who would replace Taiwan's semiconductor industry, and would the highly skilled Taiwanese fabrication technicians continue to work at their current levels if they suddenly came under Chinese communist control?

This is all about maintaining influence and relevance in a changing geopolitical landscape. The United States and China have pursued almost opposite innovation strategies, and now both are trying to catch up to the other. Perhaps the most significant development was found in the 2023 defense budget request submitted by US President Joe Biden: $145 billion for RDT&E (research, development, test, and evaluation). This was a record amount that stunned most defense industry experts, signaling that the United States has finally made a clear strategic investment in innovation as a key part of its national defense.

The paradox of Taiwan was fully revealed in May 2023, when Berkshire Hathaway disclosed that it had sold its entire stake in TSMC. Chairman Warren Buffett had bought $4.1 billion additional shares in TSMC only months earlier, but stated the reason for his sale quite clearly: "I don't like its location, and I've re-evaluated that."

Then, days later, financial markets crowned the early winners of new artificial intelligence tools like ChatGPT and competing alternatives, with California-based graphics processing unit (GPU) designer Nvidia Corporation identified as the leading supplier of chips to power our computer-sentient future. Its stock jumped by over 200 percent within days, and this American chip designer was suddenly valued at over a trillion dollars! What few mentioned was that all Nvidia's chips are made by TSMC in Taiwan.

Once more, critical technology for the future of innovation in America and the West has been outsourced. Nvidia Chief Executive Jensen Huang does not share Warren Buffett's concerns about Taiwan's present perilous state. He offered the opposite view of his supplier: "[I]n all our supply chain discussions, we feel perfectly safe." Huang added that the next generation of Nvidia's GPUs will also be made in Taiwan, while planning to source from TSMC's Arizona fabrication factories, "so we have a lot of diversity and resilience designed into our supply chain."

The reality is that those multibillion-dollar semiconductor factories in Arizona do not exist yet. For all the funding and ribbon-cutting, the United States is far from reclaiming its manufacturing, much less producing advanced microchip designs to power the future. Moreover, TSMC stated in June 2023 that the 4,500 workers required for its forthcoming factory in Arizona would be "difficult hires" due to the standard twelve-hour workdays. They added that "TSMC is about obedience [and is not] ready for America." This massive project critical to America's technological future (never mind Taiwan's essential security in locations other than the South China Sea) is very much in question, given that US unemployment rates are below 4 percent as of this writing, and the Phoenix area recently issued a building freeze due to a lack of water.

Meanwhile, China's unstoppable economy is showing serious cracks, which has inspired a citizenry that knows it has the strength to protest oppressive government decrees. Both superpowers are struggling with future economic and innovation strategies. Sadly, what the United States and China seem to agree on is the use of military threats to get what they can't make on their own.

By rethinking its economy and position worldwide, Taiwan bucked both trends and accepted practices to become an exporter and innovator, educating its people while adopting, advancing, and now dominating one of the most important industries in the world. Semiconductors have made Taiwan invaluable. Maybe too invaluable? Other world leaders, including those who are not as invaluable as they think, are so focused on this small island nation that its very existence is in question.

However powerful they may be, the United States and China must depend on their militaries while trying to promote innovation. Both nations are important, but neither fits the definition of "invaluable."

Meanwhile, Taiwan survives.

This invaluable island nation just keeps producing the semiconductors that the entire world needs—powering our consumer electronics and, ironically, the very war machines that make Taiwan a target. The world is watching, even as we all welcome and claim this one tiny nation's priceless products.

BIBLIOGRAPHY

Associated Press. "China Expands Defense Budget 7.2 Percent, Marking Slight Increase." *AP News*, March 4, 2023. https://apnews.com/article/china-defense-budget-aircraft-carriers-cdac45c8d36a47cffda68be99b7c9ee7.

BBC World News. "China and Taiwan: A Really Simple Guide." April 6, 2023. https://www.bbc.com/news/world-asia-china-59900139.

Bloomberg News. "'Irreplaceable'—Taiwan Still Dominates Chip Industry, Despite Geopolitical Turmoil." Data Center Knowledge, January 18, 2023.

https://www.datacenterknowledge.com/hardware/irreplaceable-taiwan-still-dominates-chip-industry-despite-geopolitical-turmoil.

Cohen, Ben. "The $1 Trillion Company That Started at Denny's." *Wall Street Journal*, June 1, 2023. https://www.wsj.com/articles/nvidia-ai-chips-jensen-huang-dennys-d3226926.

Dulaney, Chelsey, and Georgi Kantchev. "Russian Ruble at Weakest Level Since Early Days of Ukraine War." *Wall Street Journal*, August 14, 2023. https://www.wsj.com/articles/russian-ruble-at-weakest-level-since-early-days-of-ukraine-war-eaef275f.

The Economist. "Taiwan's Dominance of the Chip Industry Makes It More Important." March 6, 2023. https://www.economist.com/special-report/2023/03/06/taiwans-dominance-of-the-chip-industry-makes-it-more-important.

Fitzpatrick, Michael. "Chinese 'Seal Off' Taiwan, US Deploys Destroyer as War Games Unfold." *Radio France Internationale*, April 10, 2023. https://www.rfi.fr/en/international/20230410-chinese-seal-off-taiwan-us-deploys-destroyer-as-war-games-unfold.

Gallimore, Derek. "Outsource to China." *Outsource Accelerator*, March 21, 2023. https://www.outsourceaccelerator.com/articles/outsource-to-china/.

Greene, Robert, and Paul Triolo. "Will China Control the Global Internet Via Its Digital Silk Road?" Carnegie Endowment for International Peace, May 8, 2020. https://carnegieendowment.org/2020/05/08/will-china-control-global-internet-via-its-digital-silk-road-pub-81857.

Jie, Yang, and Aaron Tilley. "Apple Makes Plans to Move Production Out of China." *Wall Street Journal*, December 3, 2022. https://www.wsj.com/articles/apple-china-factory-protests-foxconn-manufacturing-production-supply-chain-11670023099.

Kinery, Emma. "TSMC to Up Arizona Investment to $40 Billion with Second Semiconductor Chip Plant." *CNBC*, December 6, 2022. https://www.cnbc.com/2022/12/06/tsmc-to-up-arizona-investment-to-40-billion-with-second-semiconductor-chip-plant.html.

Lau, Yvonne. "Chipmaker TSMC Needs to Hire 4,500 Americans at Its New Arizona Plants. Its 'Brutal' Corporate Culture Is Getting in the Way." *Fortune*, June 3, 2023. https://fortune.com/2023/06/03/tsmc-arizona-plant-jobs-salary-culture-hiring/.

Liu, John, and Paul Mozur. "Inside Taiwanese Chip Giant, a US Expansion Stokes Tensions. *New York Times*, February 22, 2023. https://www.nytimes.com/2023/02/22/technology/tsmc-arizona-factory-tensions.html.

Mathis, Joel. "The F-35 Fighter Jet's Troubled History." *The Week US*, February 13, 2023. https://theweek.com/us-military/1020858the-f-35-fighter-jets-troubled-history.

McFadden, Christopher. "US vs. Chinese Aircraft Carriers: Which Is Better?" Interesting Engineering, November 27, 2022. https://interestingengineering.com/innovation/us-vs-chinese-aircraft-carriers.

O'Meara, Sean. "US Would 'Destroy Taiwan Chip Factories If China Invaded'—BI." *Asia Financial*, March 14, 2023. https://www.asiafinancial.com/us-would-destroy-taiwan-chip-factories-if-china-invaded-bi.

Peter G. Peterson Foundation. "U.S. Defense Spending Compared to Other Countries." April 24, 2023. https://www.pgpf.org/chart-archive/0053_defense-comparison.

Qiang, Li. "Nike, Adidas, Reebok and New Balance Made in China." China Labor Watch, October 25, 2002. https://chinalaborwatch.org/nike-adidas-reebok-and-new-balance-made-in-china/.

Rand Corporation. "An Interactive Look at the US-China Military Scorecard." 2017. https://www.rand.org/paf/projects/us-china-scorecard.html.

Reuters. "Russia Doubles 2023 Defense Spending Plan as War Costs Soar." August 3, 2023. https://www.reuters.com/world/europe/russia-doubles-2023-defence-spending-plan-war-costs-soar-document-2023-08-04/#:~:text=The%20document%20provided%20a%20new,of%20its%20budget%20on%20defence.

Reyes, Max, and Jeanny Yu. "Buffett Exits TSMC While Hedge Funds Coatue, Tiger Global Buy." *Bloomberg News*, May 15, 2023. https://www.bloomberg.com/news/articles/2023-05-15/buffett-s-berkshire-offloads-last-of-tsmc-stake-in-abrupt-exit.

Statista.com. "Execution Value of Service Outsourcing Industry in China from 2016 to 2020." April 12, 2022. https://www.statista.com/statistics/1300775/china-market-size-of-service-outsourcing-industry/.

Strong, Matthew. "Nike Shifts Footwear Production from China to Vietnam." *Taiwan News*, January 5, 2022. https://www.taiwannews.com.tw/en/news/4399466.

Taiwan Today. "Veteran Tells Story of Taiwan's Semiconductor Industry." June 18, 2010. https://taiwantoday.tw/news.php?unit=6&post=9508.

3

Russia and Ukraine

Rethinking Innovation and Nations

What exactly is a nation? Can lines drawn on maps fully define a combined people, especially on an increasingly digitized planet that knows no borders? Consider the unique quandary that is Ukraine: 34 percent of Ukrainians speak Russian; 19 percent speak both Russian and Ukrainian. Though Ukraine achieved independence from the USSR on August 24, 1991, 17 percent of Ukrainians still identify themselves as "ethnically" Russian.

Dating back the 1700s and the era of Catherine the Great, Ukraine was slowly folded into Russia and remained there until the sudden collapse of the USSR. Understandably, cultural and ethnic ties still linger, making Russia's multiple invasions of Ukraine since 2014 easily branded a "liberation" by the aggressor. Confounding the question are nonstate- and state-sponsored influences that now permeate and undermine the very notion of national identities worldwide.

Not long ago, I was in a quaint café situated in Moscow's bustling Tverskaya Street. I found myself having an intriguing conversation with an elderly gentleman named Viktor. His deep-set eyes held stories from an era that shaped our modern world. Over sips of warm samovar tea, he recounted tales of a nation that once was: the mighty USSR and its glories. As the golden domes of the churches outside gleamed in the afternoon sun, Viktor's tales took me on a journey through time, painting a picture of a country that stood as a beacon of strength and innovation. As the sun faded, however, I couldn't help but note the sadness in Viktor's eyes as he recalled such promise while surrounded by so little hope for the future.

Throughout the second half of the twentieth century, the USSR was a leader in military and innovation. Without the sacrifice of some twenty-seven million Russians, Hitler's Germany would have won World War II. The United States' Manhattan Project was quickly copied by Soviet engineers, with the USSR performing its first atomic bomb test only four years later. Then, in 1957, the USSR launched Sputnik 1, the first artificial satellite in space. Americans looking to the night skies knew they'd fallen behind. The space race had begun, and the USSR was winning, sending the first man into space a decade later.

I often find myself reminding foreigners of the odds this one country defied—the land of the tsars and Bolsheviks, where winters are long and memories even longer—setting the stage for some of the world's most groundbreaking feats. Though it may be difficult to imagine the glories of the USSR today, this country—a conglomeration of ethnic groups and regional interests—was once the largest and arguably the most powerful nation on Earth, spanning one-sixth of the planet, twice the size of the United States and seventy times larger than the United Kingdom.

The triumphs of the USSR, including Ukraine as a satellite state, now live on in myths and the warm memories of people like Viktor. One of the more prescient tales to highlight the competition between the USSR and the United States is that of the pencil. As the story goes, the National Aeronautics and Space Administration (NASA) spent millions of dollars trying to invent a pen that would allow astronauts to write in zero gravity. Soviet engineers gave their cosmonauts pencils instead. But this story—typifying the practical, commonsense Soviet character versus the big-budget, ever-inventing Americans—is only partly true.

In early space tests and exploration, astronauts and cosmonauts both used pencils. NASA's concern that pencil shavings might damage sensitive aerospace equipment, or even cause a fire, justified their quest for an advanced writing tool. But, when it was revealed that American taxpayers were paying $4,382.50 (or $128.89 each) for mechanical pencils, the public outcry embarrassed NASA into finding a less expensive alternative. It took a private American citizen, Paul Fisher, spending over a million dollars of his own money to come up with the international standard for note-taking in outer space. Fisher Pen Company's "space pen" was usable both upside down and in extreme temperatures, and soon employed by both astronauts and cosmonauts. It remains one of the few things both nations ever agreed on.

This story and many others (including that of NASA's $23 million Universal Waste Management System, aka the most expensive toilet in the universe) are simultaneously awe-inspiring and nausea-inducing. Both tales illustrate the reality of innovation: multiple approaches can succeed, whether simplistic or cutting edge. Russians preferred a cheap pencil, while Americans invested in something more advanced. Both worked. It's when nations focus solely on one form of innovation that they get lost, either hitting a wall when no more cheap advancements are available or forever seeking the best and brightest, resulting in bloated budgets.

Another myth is that the USSR went bankrupt trying to keep up with American military spending. This oft-repeated belief was further cemented after former US President Ronald Reagan's death and his glorification by admirers. In reality, the USSR had not increased defense spending significantly, and was becoming more efficient in its manufacturing. What really led to the collapse of the USSR was "Demokratizatsiya." Soviet President Mikhail Gorbachev had loosened the USSR's strict authoritarian controls, even allowing multiparty elections, first in Russia, then in satellite states. With the realization of a freedom that could neither be revoked nor quelled, Lithuania voted to secede from the USSR in 1990, quickly followed by the Baltic states, then Georgia. Ukraine was late to leave "Mother" Russia, in August 1991.

Russia remains the largest nation on Earth by sheer size. But its population of 140 million is dwarfed by the United States' 330 million citizens, never mind the billions of people in China and India. And then there's the disastrous problem Russia currently faces: negative birth rates and the shorter life expectancies of its people, resulting in two million fewer Russians every three years.

Ukraine similarly suffers from shorter life expectancies and even lower birth rates than Russia. Worse, Ukraine has lost over 15 percent of its population since 1991 to emigration (to the United States and EU countries especially), dropping from more than fifty million to forty-one million today. The break-up of the USSR, while shocking and depressing to most Russians—economically and psychologically—also left its satellite states struggling to build new governments, economies, and unique national identities on their own. Many Ukrainians view being part of the greater USSR as "the good old days."

However, for some with the right connections, there was never a better time than after the USSR's collapse. Aligned with the new leaders of Russia and Ukraine, a handful of oligarchs became billionaires overnight as government-owned oil, mining, manufacturing, telecommunications, transportation, and even military operations were divided up between comrades. A gilded age had come to eastern Europe as a select few embraced capitalism while the rest were left to struggle, no longer supported by the communist state.

A thorough and rather astonishing 2003 study by the World Bank revealed how quickly oligarchs came to dominate all of Russia. Parsing 1,700 companies in 45 sectors of the Russian economy, the World Bank identified 27 individual oligarchs who controlled 42 percent of all employment in Russia and 39 percent of all annual sales—both domestically and in total exports. In addition, these oligarchs partnered with each other in multiple sectors for even greater control, with the Moscow Group of Seven and the Team of Four enjoying unparalleled wealth in Russia, exceeding $700 million USD each. And this was in 2003!

This World Bank study is now quaint, capturing this singular moment in Russia's economic tumult, with few winners and so many losers. Some of those oligarchs would soon disappear from all lists. Boris Yeltsin led Russia into its brave new era of capitalism until 1999, then Vladimir Putin became president. Put mildly, maintaining the friendship of the former KGB agent who was now in charge of Russia could be lethal.

Ukraine became known as "the sick man of Europe" after its jubilant independence in 1991. While 92 percent of Ukrainians approved of departing the USSR, the realities were rather harsh. Ever dependent on imported Russian oil and gas, government corruption was rampant, and Ukraine became one of the poorest former Soviet states, focused on an agrarian economy and dependent on foreign aid. The new nation couldn't afford to lose much, yet its economy contracted by double digits from 1991 to 1996, with hyperinflation, production declines, and mass unemployment making things worse.

But Ukrainians have character and verve; they are tough, used to struggling, and operate in a shadow economy that can't be measured. This is the most frugal of all innovation: when people know their leaders are so corrupt, they simply create their own alternate products and trade. Soviet-era aircraft components, helicopters, electronics, and pharmaceutical manufacturing continued to operate, some even thriving as Russia and other neighboring states needed spare parts and expertise.

Strangely, the rise of the oligarchs helped Ukraine emerge from authoritarian communism into a semifunctional democracy. By the early 2000s, the six richest Ukrainians were former Soviet oligarchs, and all were in the metallurgy industry. These men demanded greater efficiency, better governance, more exporting, and some basic business dictum. The Orange Revolution brought effective leadership that at last acknowledged the nation was in a deep recession and reforms were required. Progress was incredibly slow, as foreign banks brought the concept of credit to Ukraine, and a sudden demand for metals and chemicals (manufactured with cheap Russian oil) gave Ukraine a functioning economy. Ukraine's role as the "breadbasket of Europe" also helped: it supplied Russia and western Europe with millions of metric tons of hay and wheat.

A true success story, Ukraine's annual growth soon matched Russia's. The European Union (EU) and China purchased over half of its exports, while its famous "black earth" attracted serious agribusiness investment. Instead of only six oligarchs, hundreds, then thousands, of Ukrainians were finally experiencing true wealth, while millions more enjoyed gainful employment. By 2009, a middle class was emerging in Ukraine.

Then Viktor Yanukovych was elected Ukraine's president in 2010. Unmasked too late as a Russian collaborator, the new president promoted nationalism, privatizing sectors and companies that were finally functioning and profitable. Far-right leaders touted patriotism and national pride while pointing to the "good old days" of the USSR as a reason to cut ties with the EU and again embrace Russia. The whiplash was severe, and Ukraine's economy imploded. The people revolted and antigovernment demonstrations turned into riots.

In February 2014, President Yanukovych fled his country (betrayed, in hindsight), later reappearing in Russia. By then, Russian soldiers lacking insignia as "official" foreign troops were already infiltrating key positions across the Crimean Peninsula. Chaos reigned as Ukrainian troops stayed in their garrisons, their leaders naively hoping that the world, witnessing such blatant aggression by Russia, would act and assist. But the United Nations, and the rest of the world, demurred. Crimea was lost within one month.

Russia seized critical ports, military bases, and even the Ukrainian naval headquarters under the auspices of "protecting Russian citizens" in Ukraine. A puppet leader was put in place in Crimea and a rigged referendum election was held in March. While the West and Kyiv condemned the brazenness, Russia officially reintegrated Crimea. About twenty-five thousand Ukrainians were evacuated as the world voiced its disapproval while offering loans, but no military aid.

As aggressive as Putin has been, and as clearly focused on rebuilding the glory days of the USSR, his country was and is facing serious long-term problems. In addition to a shrinking population, Russia has grown stagnant under its authoritarian rule, with no competition, select oligarchs controlling business, and a gross dependence on oil exports. US President Barack Obama put it bluntly in 2016: "They [Russia] are a smaller country, they are a weaker country; their economy doesn't produce anything that anybody wants to buy except oil and gas and arms. They don't innovate."

None of this was news to Russia and Putin, so offsetting America's strategic and R&D advantages has been a priority. Since 2012, the Russian Foundation for Advanced Research Projects (known as the FPI domestically) has tried to imitate the vaunted American DARPA (Defense Advanced Research Project Agency) to invent high-payoff technologies, especially for defense. DARPA "invented" the internet and the global positioning system (GPS), as well as myriad defense systems, and is now leading research into robotics and artificial intelligence (and more defense systems), often in tandem with American companies. Russia is playing catch-up even as it quickly falls behind. With far less money to invest, Russia's FPI is betting on AI, robotics, unmanned underwater vehicles, and "directed energy" weapons to leapfrog over its enemies. Disruptive innovation is Russia's only hope.

This won't be easy: Not only does Russia not have a single MBA program, but its minuscule 1 percent of GDP investment into R&D annually will not foster any real scientific or technological advancements, which are critical for basic research and sustaining innovation. China and the United States average 2.5 percent annual investment into research and development, with economies ten times the size of Russia's. This is why the FPI is so critical for innovation, in military armaments especially, for Putin. Russia does have an impressive rocketry program that is still utilized by many nations to launch satellites and astronauts, with both Boeing and Lockheed Martin reliant on the Russia's RD-180 engine for their Atlas V rockets. SpaceX has made major breakthroughs in reusable rockets, yet its founder, Elon Musk, still praises Russian rockets as "a great engine." But even these advances date back to the former USSR.

As for military innovation, a new "hypersonic" missile was recently revealed by FPI and Putin, touted as impossible to shoot down, and then quickly copied by China. The United States has tried to develop its own hypersonic missile, but reported problems with basic accuracy and controls, so questions have been raised about Russia's newest weapon and its effectiveness. The second-largest exporter of military equipment, arms, and weapons, Russia sells to thirty-seven different countries, totaling tens of billions of US dollars annually. But even this industry has collapsed under Putin, with sales dropping by one-third over the past five years. Due to international sanctions against Russia for multiple invasions of its neighbors, as well as a lack of any real innovation or advances, Russia's customers are turning to America, France, and China for their military needs.

Oil remains Russia's cash cow, but the price per barrel must remain above $60 for Russia to make a profit. During the COVID-19 pandemic, when all industry and travel was paused, oil was trading in the negative. Russia couldn't give away its prized export. But during a crisis—an invasion of Crimea or another Middle Eastern conflict—when market jitters send oil prices skyrocketing, Russia profits enormously. Putin has played this game for so long that a "created crisis," such as turning off natural gas pipelines to Europe or any country that dares question his actions or policies, can be effective, especially in the winter months. Backed by what most consider a leading military, Russia uses oil to get what it wants.

Foreshadowing the current chaos in Ukraine, during conflicts with Chechnya and Georgia in the 1990s, military experts noted that the Russian military simply wasn't up to snuff. Serious design issues, deadly vulnerabilities, aged equipment and munitions, poorly trained troops . . . how to explain so many problems with Russia's long-feared military?

The answer: graft. Kickbacks to oligarchs from contractors, ministry officials siphoning off or outright stealing funding intended for troops, and infighting between leaders longing for Putin's approval had slowly deteriorated the country's war footing. Some estimate that as much as 50 percent of spending intended for the Russian military goes to graft, and this shortfall in R&D investment and innovation for troops and equipment became sorely evident when Russia again invaded Ukraine.

On February 24, 2022, almost exactly eight years after seizing Crimea without firing a shot, Russian troops (many lacking official insignias, as before) invaded Ukraine. And the entire world again watched. A forty-mile Russian military column was headed to attack Ukraine's capital, Kyiv, and it seemed this invasion would end as quickly as the one in Crimea. Then something astonishing happened: a small team of Ukrainians using quad all-terrain vehicles and drones totally halted the invasion.

Utilizing frugal innovation for defense, thirty Ukrainians (special ops soldiers and farmers) equipped only with sniper rifles, night vision, and remotely operated mines and drones showed the world that the Russian military was sorely lacking. Graft and corruption certainly played a part, as Russia's mechanized trucks and troop-carriers with bullet- and bomb-proof tires proved to be highly vulnerable. Obviously, a Russian oligarch or commander had found the cheapest tires available and then pocketed the difference, resulting in a forty-mile military column being halted by a few flat tires.

Russia's subpar innovation over the past few decades, combined with authoritarian leadership and a lack of competition under a handful of oligarchs, have undermined its military effectiveness. Meanwhile, Ukraine (never a true innovator) had wisely planned for another Russian invasion after Crimea and was ready. Aided by American intelligence and European allies, this agrarian, at times corrupt, former Soviet state exposed Russia as lacking on the battlefield.

The results have been devastating for both countries. Yet Ukraine is holding its ground and realizing far more success than during the loss of Crimea. The differences are critical: Ukraine's current president isn't secretly loyal to Russia, and Ukrainian troops are using creativity and innovation, mostly supplied by foreign allies, to counter the poorly trained, ill-equipped Russian invaders. Even Russia's newest weapon, the impossible-to-shoot-down hypersonic missile, is being exposed as more bluster than devastating weapon. Inaccurate and traceable by air defenses, Russia's entire arsenal, old and new, is faltering in Ukraine.

Remarkably, even Putin has admitted the gravity of this situation. When Ukraine launched a counteroffensive in June 2023, Russia's president acknowledged that "Moscow's troops are facing shortages of modern weapons." He then expressed hope that "the country's military industry will soon be able to satisfy growing demand."

May 2023 drone attacks on the Kremlin and on affluent neighborhoods around Moscow have made all Russians understand the new face of warfare. This will get even uglier; the critical Kakhovka Dam in Ukraine was bombed soon after, causing a massive civilian and environmental crisis, with both countries blaming each other.

Ukrainian President Volodymyr Zelenskyy is now a wartime leader. His citizens-turned-soldiers are stymieing Russian troops throughout Ukraine. And the situation only gets worse for Russia and its troops. We are witnessing in real time the evolution of warfare—which, sadly, is often when the greatest innovations occur.

Antitank bazookas made in the United Kingdom have further frustrated Russian troops, which has led to new warfare tactics. British troops are now training on electronic bicycles, or e-bikes, to move soldiers faster over rough terrain, armed with shoulder-fired missiles and these same antitank bazookas. The Cold War may have built a ridiculous stockpile of weapons and nuclear bombs, but it takes a real war for true innovation in military armaments and tactics to take great leaps, for good or ill.

Submersible drones are already here. In 2023, Ukraine used them to detonate Russian ships in the Black Sea. However advanced, this new weapon isn't a far cry from Bushnell's "Turtle," which attacked the HMS *Eagle* in New York Harbor in 1776. Designed by Yale graduate David Bushnell and shaped like an egg, boasting a boring device with detachable mine, the first submarine attack during wartime was a failure, mostly because the hull of the British ship was too hard to drill into. Today's submersible drones are far more effective, easily cloaked underwater, and able to attack under the darkness of night. When these exciting new drones start launching torpedoes into the abyss, if they aren't already, we will want to be worried.

The basic rules of warfare are currently being written. Defying accepted military strategy, the United States and its allies have broadcast intelligence reports on Russian troop movements, normally top-secret information. US President Joe Biden is walking a tightrope in Ukraine, trying to offer support without starting World War III. Financial and military aid have been ongoing, with the United States giving $75 billion, the European Union $30 billion, the United Kingdom $10 billion, Germany $7 billion, and Japan $6 billion (according to the most recent available figures in April 2023). Moreover, priceless military intelligence and analysis are being shared publicly and openly, which has helped to debunk Russian propaganda while giving Ukrainian troops real-time help.

Putin's go-to strategy of using crises to increase influence and oil profits isn't working this time, either. When Russia threatened to cut off western Europe's oil and natural gas supplies, the United States promptly started exporting its own oil reserves to allies, offsetting shortfalls. Price caps on Russia's oil sales were put in place in December 2022 by pro-Ukrainian allies, which has limited Putin's influence and profits. With Russian oil now pegged at $60 per barrel, Putin isn't making a profit on oil exports, and loses money when selling to China and India because those countries have demanded deep discounts for taking on the risk of doing business with the sanctioned state.

Globally, Russia's invasion of Ukraine has broad implications. Uninvolved countries are being affected, as Saudi Arabia is no longer the leading supplier of oil to China or India, due to Russia's discounting. This has created a troubling new relationship between China and Russia, as rumors fly about China (and North Korea) supplying Russia with arms.

Iran has also emerged as an important player, with its Shahed drones proving highly effective in attacks on Ukrainian cities and citizens. While Iran's drone technology was stolen from the United States and Israel a decade ago, the rogue nation has rapidly advanced its systems, and the world has taken notice. Most troubling are the hundreds of new "suicide" attack drones seen on the battlefield; these were built in Iran and shipped across the Caspian Sea for use by Russian forces, mostly to terrorize Ukrainian civilians. These "uncrewed aerial vehicles" (UAVs) clearly show a deep partnership between Iran and Russia, with some intelligence reports suggesting that Iran is assisting Russia in building a drone manufacturing facility inside Russia. This would be an entirely new paradigm, with the once-powerful Russian state now reliant on another dictatorship for advances in military technology. Not to be outdone, North Korea announced its "full support" to Russia in June 2023, with an official visit by Kim Jong-Un in August, which highlights how the invasion in Ukraine has both cemented old allegiances and forged new ones.

Perhaps the most troubling pattern to emerge from the invasion of Ukraine is the rise of the Wagner Group. These Russian mercenaries, once led by oligarch Yevgeny Prigozhin, have taken the lead in specific attacks in Ukraine, especially during the 2023 standoff in Bakhmut. A symptom of the withering away of nation-states, the primacy of companies is now seen as more efficient than governments, especially when it comes to clandestine operations for which a government would rather not publicly take direct responsibility. The Wagner Group is an extension of Putin's Russia, mostly active in controlling African diamond, gold, and precious metal mines, so this trend is being watched very closely. Interestingly, when a Russian defense minister demanded in June 2023 that "volunteer formations" must sign contracts with the ministry, Wagner boss Prigozhin refused, brashly remarking that the ministry "cannot properly manage military formation." A plane with Prigozhin aboard crashed in Russia's Tver region on August 23, 2023, with President Putin stating that the Wagner Group's late leader was "a talented person" who made "serious mistakes in life."

The Wagner Group is independent of Russia, at least according to its late leader, and Russian military leaders have lost much credibility on the Ukrainian battlefield. This serious split highlights the perils of using mercenaries in lieu of troops sanctioned and supported by the government. How "independent" can hired guns become before they turn on their benefactor? Mercenaries have a basic "cost per soldier" calculation that some view as being equal to that of state-regulated military combatants. Yet this math doesn't quite compute when factoring in the actual costs of training and retaining soldiers long-term, not to mention loyalties, especially in the new geopolitical landscape.

The reality worldwide—and particularly in the case of the Russian invasion of Ukraine—is that war is incredibly costly. In lives and treasure, the use of force is emerging as the worst option, and grossly redundant, due to digitization. Digital ambassadors are now the norm, with the EU setting up diplomatic offices in San Francisco for greater interaction with, and influence over, high-tech leaders. Meanwhile, China has established unofficial "police stations" around the world to monitor dissidents and, of course, gain intelligence. Information warfare may seem nonlethal, and it is more cost-effective and saves lives, compared to the environmental damage caused by bombs, mines, and sunken ships laden with oil.

We won't know the extent of top-secret use of state-sponsored spies and hackers (or nonstate-sponsored ones) in Ukraine, by Russia or China or anyone else (corporations included), until long after the battlefields have grown silent. But there are clues. An anonymous Ukrainian hacker was able to steal hundreds of crypto wallets (Bitcoin, among others) from Russian security agencies in 2023, then sent the funds to aid services in Ukraine. Denial of service (DNS) attacks are the norm, crippling intelligence networks, while disinformation has become a useful real-time weapon on the battlefield, with false intelligence on troop movements confusing Russian troops in unknown territories.

Obviously, increased digitization worldwide won't end all wars, nor will it invalidate mercenaries. The rise of megacorporations operating in myriad countries only underscores the devolving of nation-states. Notably, many corporations are defying international sanctions by continuing to operate in Russia and supply products, military included. And, as the Russia–Ukraine conflict continues to rage, it appears to be a war between all—by proxy among and between nation-states, stateless sponsors, international organizations, known and unknown individuals, and corporations with the capital to employ mercenaries and ignore sanctions. Adding to the chaos is a growing domestic revolt within Russia, with disenchanted locals and soldiers aiding Ukraine by attacking Russian bases, military suppliers, and manufacturing plants inside the country.

We are all witnessing the future of warfare in real time, including tanks and hackers, unmanned drones (aerial and submersible), and catastrophic attacks on civilians. Unsurprisingly, China has emerged as the chief broker to end the Ukraine–Russia conflict. Further cementing its global influence, China is replacing the United States and the United Kingdom as peacemakers, however effectively. Saudi Arabia offered to host these peace negotiations between Ukraine and Russia, which highlights the kingdom's new leadership and role in global instead of purely regional Middle Eastern affairs.

When this war ends, a global transfer of power not seen in over eighty years will take place. Russia has undermined its own future, wasting munitions and treasure, never mind whatever international respect it may still possess. Critically, Russia has also halted any innovation other than in warfare, including its development of artificial intelligence and R&D.

Ukraine, on the other hand, has all the hallmarks of a future regional power. Its breadbasket is only rivaled by America's Great Plains, producing grain, hay, and wheat, feeding tens of millions worldwide. Is it any wonder that Russia immediately tried to control Ukraine's grain supplies, negotiating trade deals with Turkey and other countries to sell what they'd stolen? Multinational agribusiness leaders could advance Ukraine's crops and yield quickly, with these innovations underwriting the country's future and regional influence. Additionally, the invasion has sparked new industries, most notably the military. Backed by eager allies, Ukraine's postwar future will be bright. Then there are the millions of Ukrainians who have left their home country for the promise of returning elsewhere, which Israel proved to be a strategic advantage in its birth and growth. From military to tech and cyber companies, metallurgy, and transport, Ukraine may emerge from this war as a stronger country, and certainly more unified with a true national identity.

As for Russia and its future, both hinge on Putin. After twenty years of authoritarian rule, economic decline, corruption, graft, and now total dependence on oil exports—instead of its history of proud innovation—perhaps the people of Russia will rise up and reclaim their country. Putin is an isolated leader, insulated from outside advice and criticism, and the history of such leaders—including Napoleon, Hussein, and Gaddafi—doesn't bode well for a peaceful transition.

Let this disgraceful invasion make us all wiser and more hopeful for a brighter day when diplomacy halts wars before they begin. This was not Russia's first invasion of Ukraine, but it must be the last. Russia's and China's economies are struggling due to this errant invasion and poor economic policies. The greatest fear must be acknowledged: two of the world's superpowers, both armed with nuclear weapons, joining the fray. Worse, add Iran and North Korea to this eastern bloc (as I write this in the first week of November 2024 North Korean soldiers have been recruited and deployed by Russia on the Ukranian front), and we will have a new Cold War of chaos, with state and nonstate actors acting both in concert and independently. This is akin to ancient kings and warlords, Mongol hordes and tribes attacking without control or strategy, only assorted self-interests, decimating their neighbors until the entire world is bedlam.

This chapter is not yet written, yet its lessons cannot be ignored.

BIBLIOGRAPHY

Armstrong, Martin. "The Countries Committing the Most Aid to Ukraine." Statista.com, September 22, 2023. https://www.statista.com/chart/28489/ukrainian-military-humanitarian-and-financial-aid-donors/.

BBC News. "Putin Breaks Silence over Prigozhin's Reported Death." August 24, 2023. https://www.bbc.com/news/world-europe-66609678.

BBC News. "Ukraine in Maps: Tracking the War with Russia." November 15, 2023. https://www.bbc.com/news/world-europe-60506682.

Brittanica. "The Crisis in Crimea and Eastern Ukraine." Accessed May 7, 2023, https://www.britannica.com/place/Ukraine/The-crisis-in-Crimea-and-eastern-Ukraine.

Chrysopoulos, Philip. "How the Mines of Laurion Changed Ancient Athens and the World." *Greek Reporter*, May 21, 2023. https://greekreporter.com/2022/05/30/mines-laurion-athens-western-civilization/.

Conway, Madeline. "Obama Dismisses Russia as a 'Weaker Country.'" Politico, December 16, 2016. https://www.politico.com/story/2016/12/obama-russia-weaker-country-232759.

ConnecticutHistory.org. "The Turtle Submarine." September 6, 2021. https://connecticuthistory.org/the-turtle-submarine-today-in-history/.

Curtin, Ciara. "Fact or Fiction?: NASA Spent Millions to Develop a Pen That Would Write in Space, Whereas the Soviet Cosmonauts Used a Pencil." *Scientific American*, December 20, 2006. https://www.scientificamerican.com/article/fact-or-fiction-nasa-spen/.

The Economist. "Russia's Population Nightmare Is Going to Get Even Worse." March 4, 2023. https://www.economist.com/europe/2023/03/04/russias-population-nightmare-is-going-to-get-even-worse.

Guriev, Sergei, and Andrei Rachinsky. "The Role of Oligarchs in Russian Capitalism." *Journal of Economic Perspectives* 19, no. 1 (Winter 2005): 131–50. https://pubs.aeaweb.org/doi/pdfplus/10.1257/0895330053147994.

Halsall, Paul. "Ancient History Sourcebook, Herodotus: Xerxes Invades Greece, from *The Histories*." Fordham University, August 2000. https://sourcebooks.fordham.edu/ancient/herodotus-xerxes.asp.

Ivanova, Ievgeniia. "Why Many Ukrainians Speak Russian as Their First Language." *The Conversation*, October 12, 2022. https://theconversation.com/why-many-ukrainians-speak-russian-as-their-first-language-190856.

Jackson, Jon. "Putin Admits Russia Doesn't Have Enough Modern Weapons." *Newsweek*, June 9, 2023. https://www.newsweek.com/putin-admits-russia-doesnt-have-enough-modern-weapons-1805665.

Jankowicz, Mia. "Ukraine Hit Russia's Navy Base in Crimea So Hard That It Is Likely Pulling Some Missions Back to Safer Waters." *Business Insider*, October 2, 2023. https://www.businessinsider.com/russia-moving-black-sea-fleet-operations-away-crimea-uk-ukraine-2023-10.

Jankowski, Dominik P. "Russia and the Technological Race in an Era of Great Power Competition." Center for Strategic and International Studies, September 14, 2021. https://www.csis.org/analysis/russia-and-technological-race-era-great-power-competition.

Karnazes, Dean. "The Real Pheidippides Story," *Runner's World*, December 6, 2016. https://www.runnersworld.com/runners-stories/a20836761/the-real-pheidippides-story/.

Kulu, H., S. Christison, C. Liu, and J. Mikolai. "The War, Refugees, and the Future of Ukraine's Population." *Population, Space and Place* 29 (2023): e2656. https://doi.org/10.1002/psp.2656.

Lefkowitz, Ben. "Backdoor Negotiations Over Ukraine Would Be a Disaster." *Foreign Policy*, August 3, 2023. https://foreignpolicy.com/2023/08/03/ukraine-war-negotiations-russia-china-saudi-african-union-diplomacy/.

Mason, Jeff, and Steve Holland. "Russia Received Hundreds of Iranian Drones to Attack Ukraine." *Reuters*, June 9, 2023. https://www.reuters.com/world/europe/russia-has-received-hundreds-iranian-drones-attack-ukraine-white-house-2023-06-09/.

McCallion, Jane. "10 Amazing DARPA Inventions: How They Were Made and What Happened to Them." *IT Pro*, June 15, 2020. https://www.itpro.com/technology/34730/10-amazing-darpa-inventions.

National Aeronautics and Space Administration. "Sputnik and the Dawn of the Space Age." Updated October 10, 2007. https://history.nasa.gov/sputnik.html.

New Voice of Ukraine. "Unexpected Failure of Russian Hackers and Ukraine's Ascendant IT Expertise." December 23, 2022. https://english.nv.ua/nation/unexpected-failure-of-russian-hackers-and-ukraine-s-ascendant-it-expertise-50293089.html.

Office of the Historian. "The Collapse of the Soviet Union." Foreign Service Institute, US Department of State. Last updated April 8, 2018. https://history.state.gov/milestones/1989-1992/collapse-soviet-union.

Pifer, Steven. "Crimea: Six Years After Illegal Annexation." Brookings Institute, March 17, 2020. https://www.brookings.edu/blog/order-from-chaos/2020/03/17/crimea-six-years-after-illegal-annexation/.

Richman, Barry M. "Innovation Problems in Soviet Industry," *Management International* 3, no. 6 (1963): 67–79. https://www.jstor.org/stable/40225538.

Sample, Ian. "AI-Powered Drone Beats Human Champion Pilots." *The Guardian*, August 30, 2023. https://www.theguardian.com/technology/2023/aug/30/ai-powered-drone-beats-human-champion-pilots.

Shinkman, Paul D. "How Russian Corruption Is Foiling Putin's Army in Ukraine." *US News & World Report*, August 31, 2022. https://www.usnews.com/news/world-report/articles/2022-08-31/how-russian-corruption-is-foiling-putins-army-in-ukraine.

Shoaib, Alia. "An Elite Ukrainian Drone Unit on Quad Bikes Ambushed Russian Forces, Helping to Defeat Putin's Plan to Capture Kyiv." *Business Insider*, April 3, 2022. https://www.businessinsider.com/elite-ukrainian-drone-unit-on-quad-bikes-ambushed-russian-forces-the-guardian-2022-4.

Smith, Helena. "Search on for Secret of Greek Sea Battle." *The Guardian*, June 19, 2005. https://www.theguardian.com/world/2005/jun/20/research.highereducation.

Sor, Jennifer. "China Is Snapping Up Russian Oil at the Steepest Discount in Months as EU Scrambles to Keep a Lid on Moscow's Energy Income." *Business Insider*, December 7, 2022. https://markets.businessinsider.com/news/commodities/russia-oil-price-cap-espo-china-discount-crude-eu-ban-2022-12.

Starkey, Jerome. "British Troops Trained with Ukraine's Tactic of Bikes and Bazookas to Take Out Tanks." *The Sun* (US edition), July 30 2023. https://www.the-sun.com/news/8726292/british-troops-ukraine-bikes-bazookas-take-out-tanks/.

Sutela, Pekka. "The Underachiever: Ukraine's Economy Since 1991." Carnegie Endowment for International Peace, March 9, 2012. https://carnegieendowment.org/2012/03/09/underachiever-ukraine-s-economy-since-1991-pub-47451.

Tayeb, Zahra, and Sam Tabahriti. "Elon Musk Says the Russian Rocket Engines Boeing and Lockheed Martin Use Are 'Great,' Amid the Country's Decision to Stop Supplying the US." *Business Insider*, March 27, 2022. https://www.businessinsider.com/elon-musk-russian-rocket-engines-great-boeing-lockheed-martin-2022-3.

US Department of the Treasury. "The Price Cap on Russian Oil: A Progress Report." May 18, 2023. https://home.treasury.gov/news/featured-stories/the-price-cap-on-russian-oil-a-progress-report.

Warsaw Institute. "High Oil Prices Make Russian Production More Profitable." December 20, 2021. https://warsawinstitute.org/high-oil-prices-make-russian-production-profitable/.

World Bank. "Russia's Uphill Struggle with Innovation." September 17, 2018. https://www.worldbank.org/en/news/opinion/2018/09/17/russias-uphill-struggle-with-innovation.

Part II

THE DANGERS OF BEING OUTSIDE THE GLOBAL INNOVATION ECOSYSTEM

4

North Korea

Outside by Choice

North Korea epitomizes frugal innovation, and fully by choice. Self-isolated since the early 1950s, there is no real chance for organic evolution under the dictatorship of the Kim regime. When clients dare ask me how not to innovate and fail, I simply say: "North Korea."

Ironically, both Israel and North Korea emerged at the same time; both were impoverished countries with few allies, both nations born from war. As detailed in chapter 1, the difference is that Israel chose to open itself up to immigrants and allies, fostering, then fully embracing, innovation and exports to defend itself. Conversely, North Korea has almost glaciated itself into one geological era that it can't escape. Therefore, this case study on North Korea is the clearest example of the focus of part 2 of this book: the dangers of being outside the global innovation ecosystem.

In its present state, North Korea suffers the whims of multiple Kim descendants: Kim Il-Sung, his son Kim Jong-Il, and now the grandson, Kim Jong-Un. Allies such as China and (at times) Russia have grown wary of the unpredictable personalities leading North Korea. Meanwhile, the people of North Korea have been taught to worship their leaders from a young age, while simultaneously being indoctrinated with utter hatred toward the United States.

"We can't develop because of American sanctions."

"You say isolated. We say self-reliant. That's our ideology. That's how we weather economic crises caused by America."

These are the words of North Koreans. Not international propaganda, but the real people sharing their views of their communist country, including their seventy-plus years of war with the United States. South Korea never signed the 1953 Korean Armistice Agreement between North Korea, China, and the United States so, technically, the Korean War has never ended. This is especially true of North Korea–economically, politically, culturally, and technologically.

"Our hometown has fourteen universities. Does your hometown have as many?" This is yet another proud declaration by an unnamed (by request) North Korean.

Yes, North Korea may have fourteen universities in a single city, but they are all designed and molded by the Kim regime and populated by a loyal citizenry who perform their duties as assigned by the regime. There is no creativity, no alternative techniques or beliefs, no exposure to external ideas or recent advances. Even young children are taught to obey the regime over their own parents, while critical thinking is rejected.

North Korea is the antithesis of innovation, and a case study that I regularly cite of how not to manage technology, never mind govern.

Still, the unique societal structure, as well as mental programming, of North Koreans after seventy-five years of being ruled by a single dictatorial family must be understood. Parsing reality from propaganda is essential. The rare outsider with an opportunity to visit and get to know North Korea must always quote its isolated people on the condition of anonymity. Citizens who speak candidly about their leadership are regularly sentenced to three years in prison camps, which amounts to a death sentence due to the camps' notorious severity, with starvation and executions the norm.

"Mostly, people criticize ['Supreme Leader'] Kim Jong-Un for being a businessman. People say that he acts the same as us but takes away our money. The little man uses his head to suck up money like a little vampire."

Such a statement would surely condemn the speaker to a prison camp, or worse. The Kim regime utilizes a unique technique to control twenty-six million North Koreans. One family member's criticism of the regime will result in prison time with no ability to appeal; additionally, all their sisters, brothers, in-laws, children, and parents are equally punished, and it can go on forever. Three, even eight, generations of punishment are the norm.

There are fifty-one different classes in North Korea, based on a caste system known as *songbun*—the sociopolitical classification that determines the status of everyone. Basically, whatever class your family is in, is the class in which you and your children will remain. One's distinct caste is a given destination upon birth, ignoring what the individual may want.

Any dictatorship requires unquestioned control, as well as one other critical component: an enemy.

"Everyone dislikes America. We say the reason for us living in poverty is because America split us and sealed us off [from South Korea]."

Kim Il-Sung was a legendary leader of communist guerrillas fighting Japan during its occupation of the Korean Peninsula in the 1930s. Backed by the Soviet Union, the Kim dynasty founded the Democratic People's Republic of Korea in 1948. On June 25, 1950, Kim sent some seventy-five thousand North Korean troops into South Korea. The resulting Korean War was a brief but bloody draw. While South Korea gained over fifteen hundred square miles of territory between 1950 and 1953, the partitioning of the Korean Peninsula remained at the thirty-eighth parallel afterward.

China backed North Korea, and the United States branded its support of South Korea as a necessary measure to stop the spread of communism. The Korean War wasn't a high point for Americans accustomed to victory, especially following World War II. Conditions were brutal, North Korea was utterly inhospitable to foreign invaders, and the sacrifices of its people were rather shocking. Casualties were much higher than during World War II, especially for civilians, and the war ended in an uneasy standoff.

North Korean propaganda followed the armistice, and even the actual deaths during the war were inflated. North Korea claimed the incredibly high number of nearly three million deaths and casualties. What the regime didn't report was that nearly eight hundred thousand of its people fled to South Korea. Newfound documents prove that North Korea lost an extraordinary 20 percent of its total population from 1950 to 1953, but these losses weren't all due to war. Civilian casualties were incredibly high, at over one million, yet nearly one-third of the regime's claimed losses were a result of North Koreans emigrating over enemy lines.

The United States isn't above propaganda and it, too, manipulated the number of American soldiers lost in North Korea: 54,260 is the Pentagon's commonly published death toll for the Korean War. It has since been discovered that the Pentagon included "all other deaths" of American soldiers from 1950 to 1953 in its Korean War reporting. The real number is 36,914 American deaths in North Korea; over 17,000 "other deaths" did not actually occur on the Korean Peninsula.

Agrarian and autocratic, North Korea has long been a monarchy, with its people resigned to inequality. Kim Il-Sung promised massive change: No landowners, no rich, no poor, nothing but the state. The state would own everything and provide everything, with all people being equal, relegated to their castes. Confiscation of private lands and wealth, even cattle and belongings, began in earnest. The *songbun* caste system went into full effect and all North Koreans were segmented and divided, leaving zero room for individuality, and only the Kim family as the state.

"Everything would be free, no trading, no ownership, no private property, you can't own a home, a cow, a car. . . . There was not much of a battle, people gave everything to the regime. And, if you questioned it, people got executed," offers Yeonmi Park, whose family fled from North Korea to China in 2007. "My father was a parliamentary member, so we were middle class. I never saw a shower in my life. We don't even have a word for shower. We didn't have running water. We had to go to the river. . . . If you weren't dying of starvation in the nineties, that meant you were wealthy."

However fierce in government control and battle, North Korea is impoverished regarding its frugal innovation. Ignoring the centralized wealth and comforts enjoyed by the Kim regime, North Korea's utter reliance on Chinese aid and trade leaves it sorely lacking. This has hardened its people, sharing in their struggle, their anger focused on evil America, with accomplishments by the regime lauded as major points of national pride.

Of course there is no World Wide Web, no foreign news, and any internet or communications are strictly controlled. The Kim regime is always right, and very successful! North Korea won the FIFA World Cup in 2010. In fact, it didn't, but don't tell that to North Koreans who celebrated their shared 1–0 victory over Brazil. Confused yet? Spain actually won the World Cup in 2010, 1–0 versus the Netherlands. The brainwashing doesn't end there: Supreme Leader Kim is immortal; he doesn't need to urinate or defecate, and every nation on Earth celebrates his birthday. You can't make this stuff up, but North Koreans believe it wholeheartedly.

Beyond controlling its people, what North Korea does incredibly well is enacting national strategies by mandate. The Kim regime understood that, without technology, it could not retain power, never mind build an economy or any wealth. Thus the Third Economic Plan was announced in 1987, boldly declaring the twenty-first century the "IT era." Hindering this massive state initiative was the fact that North Korea had been labeled a "rogue state" (along with Iran and Sudan); Western countries could not sell or provide advanced computers to North Korea. Compared to South Korea at this moment, North Korea was technologically twenty years behind.

"Focus on science and technology in building a powerful and prosperous nation" was its anthem and, with assistance from the United Nations Development Program, North Korea built its own optical cable factory in Pyongyang, then laid over a million miles of phone lines. Defense headquarters and capitals were first to be connected by fiber, with most long-distance telecommunications using conventional wire and, always, the people coming last. By the late 1990s, there were five phone lines for every hundred households, which allowed long-distance or international calls to be strictly limited.

The electronic communications system developed in North Korea is intentionally insular: a single foreign relay station in Beijing is the sole connection to the outside world. All international calls must pass through this Chinese station and, from there, AT&T has established a network for all communications with the United States and abroad. The Kim regime monitors and controls incoming and outgoing communications, going to great lengths to restrain its people, outside influences, and advances.

Still, the state did make progress. More than a hundred universities and technical schools teach science and technology in tandem to achieve its mandated goals. By the early 2000s, North Korea claimed it had a hundred thousand information technology experts, and even its own computer manufacturing factories. Highlighting the centralized control over its people, the Ministry of Higher Education holds annual Computer Olympiads to identify young talent. However, North Korea is only as effective as it allows, due to its caste system and a universal rejection of immigrants and outside ideas. Those hundred thousand IT experts may be highly touted inside the country, but they were purposely selected and trained by the regime, with no regard to skill sets or actual abilities. A lack of critical thinking renders the concept of science or further advances difficult to grasp for most. These "IT experts" have no access to other experts outside of North Korea; information sharing is discouraged, so they are cut off from any ecosystem not controlled by the regime. Overriding the very notion of communist dictatorships, the people are merely numbers to be praised in propaganda.

Software development with a focus on Microsoft Windows is standard, but so too is ideological indoctrination. All universities and technical schools, though focused on science and technology, must set aside over 40 percent of class time to further instill in students the importance of the state, the infallibility of the Kim dynasty, the risks of individuality, and the evils of America.

The internet is another matter entirely. The very nature of sharing information is a direct threat to the regime, contradicting the dictatorial and unique societal structure of North Korea. However, that doesn't mean the regime doesn't use the internet for its own interests: propaganda, corporate espionage, and hacking.

The Lazarus Group is the most infamous North Korean team of hackers. Based in a hotel over the border in China, their exposure to Chinese technical professionals has made North Korea's hackers some of the best in the world. Trained in Shenyang, China, these elite hackers use malware, spyware, and advanced techniques to inflict major international damage.

In 2014, the Lazarus Group's target was Sony Pictures; its satirical movie *The Interview* dared poke fun at Kim Jong-Un. Soon, legions of hackers had stolen confidential and rather embarrassing corporate information from Sony, which was then publicly released by a group calling itself the Guardians of Peace. Investigations have since tied these online efforts to the Lazarus Group.

In 2016, North Korean hackers stole $81 million USD from Bangladesh's national bank during a single weekend, in an "elegant" attack that few would think the supposedly undeveloped country of North Korea could devise. The hackers had used complex "phishing" techniques to infiltrate the central bank systems almost one year earlier, even altering commands to a key printer that could have notified employees of the theft in process. Stolen funds were then routed through the Philippines and made nearly untraceable. It had the makings of a major film heist: only after hackers had enjoyed a full weekend of control over the bank's systems did Bangladeshi bankers realize what was happening. They halted it before thirty-five more transfers totaling over $1 billion could be completed. Multiple bank officials resigned afterward, and all the world knew that North Korea had hackers capable of anything.

Such thefts aren't limited to cash via electronic withdrawals. In 2022 alone, North Korean hackers stole an estimated $1.7 billion worth of "virtual" currency, including $620 million from the online game Axle Infinity. From gamers to Bitcoin to sensitive government secrets, North Korea is a leader in international hacking, with no computer safe from their eager fingertips.

As for the military, the demilitarized zone (DMZ) separating North and South Korea is ever armed and active. Few countries would want to invade North Korea, yet the Kim regime remains steadfast in appearing outwardly aggressive. Kim Jong-Il launched his country into a buildup of assorted ballistic and cruise missiles, including a vast air defense system. After Jong-Il's death in 2011, his twenty-seven-year-old son Kim Jong-Un increased missile tests tenfold, both to add ICBMs to his arsenal and for worldwide attention. Most foreign intelligence observers cite domestic issues as the major reason for more launches. When there is a bad harvest or civil unrest, North Korea fires more missiles.

After gaining China's hacking expertise, then stealing some primitive forms of rocketry and missile technology, North Korea is a force that can no longer be ignored. The question must be asked: are hackers and missiles enough in today's troubled geopolitical landscape?

Hackers do not operate in silos. They learn their skills by being surrounded by technology and being able to test and then "hack" that technology. That skill set quickly becomes obsolete when new technologies are introduced. In late 2023, HSBC implemented a new quantum cryptography system, so North Korean hackers are now snookered. In order to hack any technology, one must understand it fully. Hackers need to innovate, and without fully understanding quantum computing (something North Korea definitely does not possess), novel ways to counteract or hack it are virtually impossible.

The same is true of North Korea's missile technology. Stolen technology is only as relevant as the technological ecosystem in which it operates. North Korea's current technology would be useless against the Iron Dome of Israel, which is the most visible version of the secretive US "Star Wars" air defense systems. For offensive missiles to be effective, they need to keep pace with other related innovations. This became clear once Russia launched its vaunted hypersonic missiles into Ukraine, only to discover (and be embarrassed by) how vulnerable they truly were. Anyone may "steal" or adapt primitive forms of technology, but there are much larger universes at work, which impact everything.

So when North Korea has a poor harvest, it hacks or fires its missiles. When Kim Jong-Un feels disrespected by further sanctions or a lack of response to his first missile launches, he fires more. China is North Korea's main support, offering desperately needed food when starvations peak under the brutal Kim regime, but even China has limits. The universally accepted belief is that China tolerates and assists its neighbor because it doesn't want millions of North Korean refugees flooding its borders.

Uncomfortable with the young Kim Jong-Un's lack of experience, as well as his bellicose leadership style, China has recently kept diplomatic ties unusually distant. When Kim declared that North Korea would become a nuclear superpower, China showed even greater reluctance to provide international support. Further nuclear tests have proven both provocative and grossly irresponsible, with multiple failed missile launches further provoking neighbors in the China Sea. This is an already agitated region for China, with growing tensions over Taiwan, as well as the many US military bases in Japan.

On May 31, 2023, North Korea unsuccessfully launched its first military spy satellite, and South Korean and Japanese authorities urged their people to take shelter. The failed satellite crashed into the Yellow Sea off the west coast of the peninsula, and North Korea immediately declared that it would soon launch another spy satellite. That one, launched in August 2023, also failed.

While North Korea's rockets have mostly underwhelmed, the new Chollima-1 rocket that has failed to deliver the Malligyong-1 satellite is a major step forward. This boldness, as well as the breadth of technology used, startled the region—allies included—and shows that North Korea is quickly closing several technological gaps. Exactly who is helping in these advances is open to debate.

For comparison, South Korea's GDP is $1.8 trillion. North Korea's GDP is $30 billion, or 2.2 percent of the GDP of its southern neighbor and sworn enemy. Yet North Korea devotes around 25 percent of its entire economy to its military. While this pales in comparison to American or Chinese military budgets in total dollars and yuan, it shows that North Korea seeks to develop singular, calamitous weapons, such as hypersonic missiles like Russia's or nuclear-equipped ICBMs. Clandestine and "elegant" hackers who can overtake and control other nations' computer systems undetected are already a given.

This requires money, which comes in both legal and illegal forms. China accounts for around 75 percent of North Korea's trade, while coal and other minerals find welcome markets abroad. There are illicit military deals, mostly with Iran and unknown African nations and/or companies. Unnervingly, many of these illegal arms sales are only discovered by accident. In 2016, a North Korean ship supposedly transporting construction materials was intercepted by Egypt and found to be carrying thirty thousand rocket-propelled grenades and other military parts. For whom, no one could precisely say.

On par with North Korea's hacking operations are its industries counterfeiting currency and fake pharmaceuticals. The country is the third-largest producer of opium and heroin worldwide, and its factories produce perfect replicas of high-demand drugs such as Viagra. Illegal drugs result in quick, untraceable cash, which is then funneled into military weapons.

Since North Korea has eclipsed its domestic skills and talent with rocketry and nuclear programs—evolving from frugal to disruptive today—government and corporate espionage are now necessary. Japan has reported multiple hacks, as well as bribes, originating in North Korea. More worrisome is that these attempts have targeted Japan's own secret nuclear and rocket programs. There is also growing consensus that North Korea may be working with Iran to advance both nations' nuclear programs. In reality, and on the world stage, North Korea continues to punch above its weight, despite international sanctions and the starvation of its people.

Whatever the world's ultimate solution to North Korea may be, it will be grave: for the Kim regime; for its neighbors, China and South Korea; and for its recent allies, Iran and unnamed African nations or corporations. A psychopath with nuclear weapons simply cannot be allowed.

The sudden rise of Kim Jong-Un's sister, Kim Yo-Jong, is also unnerving. Known to execute North Korean officials for questioning her (or for just "getting on her nerves"), Kim Yo-Jong is the new face of the regime and may prove more bellicose and belligerent than her brother. During the COVID-19 outbreak, Kim Yo-Jong admitted that her brother had the "high fever" (as North Korea called COVID-19) to explain his many absences from public events. When he eventually returned to public view, Kim Jong-Un showed significant weight loss and seemed physically weak, limping and needing assistance. Some intelligence sources speculate that he may be in poor health due to heavy drinking and unknown medical issues.

Interestingly, North Korea blamed its "high fever" (aka COVID-19) on leaflets dropped by air from South Korea, then reported an unbelievably low total of only seventy-four deaths. Given North Korea's substandard health care system and utter lack of any COVID testing kits, the World Health Organization reports its actual total COVID-19 cases and deaths as "unknown."

Still, from the pandemic rose Kim Yo-Jong. She has made very public appearances on behalf of North Korea at the 2018 Olympics, nuclear summits and, increasingly, statewide events. Not only was she present for multiple ICBM test launches, but Kim Yo-Jong was the only regime spokesperson after its first failed spy satellite launch in May 2023, where she declared the

Pacific Ocean a "firing range." Her brother appears to be trying to retake the bullhorn from his sister, announcing that his successor won't be Kim Yo-Jong but his daughter, ten-year-old Kim Ju Ae. "The Chosen One" will continue the Kim regime into a fourth generation, and the girl's sudden publicity seems a warning to her aunt to stand down.

Regardless of publicity stunts or missile launches, the Kim regime earns outsized international attention. Former US President Donald Trump played right into the Kim regime's game by regularly acknowledging "little rocket man." Trump even exchanged what were described as "love letters" with the despot during his term. So Kim Jong-Un's June 2023 announcement that North Korea "holds hands" with Russia, however unsettling, was no surprise. Kim offered his "full support" regarding Ukraine, which prompted an official state visit to Russia in August and public meetings with Vladimir Putin. Whether this new relationship includes armaments, technology sharing, hacking, or Russia's advanced rocketry programs, no one can say as of yet.

What no one doubts are the aims of the Kim regime: control and self-preservation. While reclaiming the public stage from his sister, Kim Jong-Un announced the need for a wall to be built along the border with South Korea. Since no South Koreans are crossing into the DMZ, it's clear that Kim Jong-Un is concerned about his own people fleeing the country. This echoes his grandfather's leadership of the communist revolution on the Korean Peninsula seventy-five years ago, invading the south and promptly losing over eight hundred thousand citizens to emigration.

Economically, North Korea's people are paying the price for the regime's quest for military might, with mass starvation, poor health care, prison camps, and an education system focused solely on the Kim regime's mythology. Most people, no matter how brainwashed or terrified, have an inherent longing to be free. North Koreans who have escaped the country learn to enjoy both choice and opportunity, liberation, less fear, and comforts like showers and more food. Not having prison camps or caste systems is rather addictive, impossible to quell once experienced—freedom is the cure for despots. It's no wonder that Kim Jong-Un wants to build a wall, and that China's greatest concern is millions of North Koreas running for its border.

As the global technological evolution accelerates, North Korea's theft and bribery model is not sustainable. North Koreans will be left farther and farther behind, especially considering the latest innovation in artificial intelligence: AI RL (reinforcement learning). When a hundred million simulations of future scenarios can be performed in an instant, one can no longer lie, cheat, or steal their way into competing against such a system. And, for every single simulation among millions, North Korea is being left further behind.

Until then, this is a rogue state by choice: stoic in its frugal innovation through all means necessary, despite isolation. Where innovation is lacking,

North Korea utilizes cybertheft and illegal trade to gain equipment and intelligence that it cannot generate domestically. Perhaps its sole opportunity is a change in policy by opening and working with others, rogue states like Iran included.

Never forget, though: North Korea's survival is equal to its threat to others. And, as long as a Kim is in charge, fear the worst.

BIBLIOGRAPHY

BBC News. "The Lazarus Heist: How North Korea Almost Pulled Off a Billion-Dollar Hack." June 21, 2021. https://www.bbc.com/news/stories-57520169.

CBS News. "How Many Americans Died in Korea?" June 5, 2020. https://www.cbsnews.com/news/how-many-americans-died-in-korea/

Cheng, Evelyn. "Five Ways North Korea Gets Money to Build Nuclear Weapons." CNBC, April 18, 2017. https://www.cnbc.com/2017/04/18/how-does-north-korea-get-money-to-build-nuclear-weapons.html.

Cho, Timothy. "Kim Jong-Un's New Border Wall Could Be a Sign That His Grip on North Korea Is Slipping." *The Guardian*, June 5, 2023. https://www.theguardian.com/commentisfree/2023/jun/05/kim-jong-un-border-wall-north-korea-technology.

Cowan, Michael. "Ordinary North Koreans Dare to Speak Out Despite Fear." *BBC News*, May 29, 2018. https://www.bbc.com/news/world-asia-44290822.

Lee, Hyung-Seog. "Information Technology Progress in North Korea and Its Prospects." In *Bytes and Bullets in Korea*, edited by Alexandrea Mansourov, 100–120. Honolulu: Asia Pacific Center for Security Studies, 2005. https://dkiapcss.edu/wp-content/uploads/2010/PDFs/Edited%20Volumes/BytesAndBullets/CH5.pdf.

Lee, Sung-Yoon, "The rise of North Korea's Most Dangerous Woman," *Telegraph*, June 8, 2023. https://www.telegraph.co.uk/world-news/2023/06/06/kim-jong-un-sister-north-korea/.

Lendon, Brad. "Why Kim Jong Un Wants You to Meet His Daughter." CNN, February 10, 2023. https://www.cnn.com/2023/02/10/asia/kim-jong-un-daughter-succession-missiles-north-korea-intl-hnk/index.html.

PBS. "Kim Il Sung." Accessed June 5, 2023. https://www.pbs.org/tpt/dictators-playbook/episodes/kim-il-sung/.

PBS News Hour. "Kim Jong Un's Sister Vows North Korea Will Make Second Attempt to Launch Spy Satellite." June 4, 2023. https://www.pbs.org/newshour/world/kim-jong-uns-sister-vows-north-korea-will-make-2nd-attempt-to-launch-spy-satellite.

Reynolds, Emma. "'We're Peaceful People': North Koreans in Their Own Words." News.com.au, November 20, 2015. https://www.news.com.au/lifestyle/real-life/news-life/were-peaceful-people-north-koreans-in-their-own-words/news-story/8e5e59dd0275f282c75793be43adc9d6.

Robertson, Phil. "North Korea's Caste System." *Human Rights Watch*, July 5, 2016. https://www.hrw.org/news/2016/07/05/north-koreas-caste-system.

South China Morning Post. "US Sanctions Chinese Men Linked to Notorious North Korean Hackers." April 25, 2023. https://www.scmp.com/news/world/united-states-canada/article/3218209us-sanctions-chinese-men-linked-notorious-north-korean-hackers.

Wilson Center. "New Evidence on North Korean War Losses." August 1, 2001. https://www.wilsoncenter.org/article/new-evidence-north-korean-war-losses.

World Health Organization. "Democratic People's Republic of Korea Situation." November 8, 2023. https://covid19.who.int/region/searo/country/kp.

5

Iran

Expelled

In late 2010, I was heading up de-mining operations along the South Iraq–Iran border. Needless to say, this was dangerous work, and I'd often find myself peering off at the dusty landscape of Basra. Among the physical ruins and remnants of wars gone by, there's a vast chasm between potential and reality.

Iran is a paradox. On one hand, it's a nation deeply embedded in regional conflicts, a state often whispered about for its dealings with Russia, North Korea, and many other rogue nonstate actors. Yet at its core is a vibrant, youthful populace, thirsty for innovation and growth.

The question is not what Iran is, but which Iran are we referring to? Is it the rogue state (already mentioned multiple times in this book) supplying Russia with deadly unmanned drones to attack Ukraine, soldiers and civilians alike? Is it the theocratic Islamic Republic that is aiding North Korea in their shared nuclear ambitions, bringing technical expertise to another isolated nation's despotic ruler? Or is it the scourge of the Middle East, spreading terrorism through nonstate actors like Hamas and clandestine operations? Yes, Iran is all the above, but it is also so much more.

Tehran isn't just Iran's political capital; it's a bustling city teeming with life, resembling major global hubs like London in hustle and verve. There are modern buildings, traffic jams, several universities, and people going about their everyday business, working normal jobs, shopping, and taking selfies. While women dress conservatively—wearing headscarves with no skin showing—Iranians do enjoy some liberties regarding their official dress codes in comparison to other Islamic nations. Self-reliant since the Western-backed Shah was ousted in September 1978, this oil-rich nation is run by clerics and hand-picked presidents laboring under severe economic sanctions that limit imports and exports. Nevertheless, Iran's leaders have made a universal mandate to become a "knowledge-based economy."

This won't be easy, according to multiple UN reports on Iran. One states: "However, unlike other middle-income countries, Iran is still largely a natural resource–based economy. Diversification is an imperative, not only because natural resources are exhaustible but also because export success in world markets increasingly demands knowledge-intensive production and innovation-based competition." That report was written in 2005. In 2021, a UNESCO report showed impressive results: "By 2020, 49 innovation accelerators had been established with private equity and 113 innovation centers had been set up in partnership with science parks and major universities."

However effective these "innovation accelerators" and "innovation centers" truly are is dubious, as Iran is hindered by its own insulation and international sanctions. Despite the government's push toward fewer competitive barriers and an openness to financial support, this latest UN report in 2021 singled out Iran's major challenge: "Despite growth in the number of master's and PhD graduates, there is a high share (39 percent) of unemployment among university graduates."

About 60 percent of Iran's eighty million people are thirty years old or younger, while its birth rate is higher than that of most developed countries. This is a good problem to have when compared to China's and Russia's negative birth rates, but Iran's leadership seems mired in a constant struggle to control its underemployed and increasingly dissatisfied youth. Ongoing protests are common, as young Iranians demand greater freedoms from the Islamic clerics who govern their lives and oversee their future aspirations. Ever teetering on the brink of a coup d'état (the hope of Iran's enemies), these revolts are quickly and forcefully quelled by the feared Islamic Revolutionary Guard Corps (IRGC), who number nearly two hundred thousand and are controlled by the regime. Monitoring civilian communications—especially social media—allows the government to arrest anyone with a dissenting voice at any moment.

Fear governs a youthful Iranian populace that is both highly educated and increasingly technical, thanks to the regime's efforts to make the country more "knowledge based." Yet most of Iran's population does not benefit from their newfound skill sets, as the country's isolation and international sanctions undermine foreign trade, thus sparking massive unemployment. This serious quandary is a threat to the regime because Iran is a rogue nation, expelled from the global innovation ecosystem due to state-sponsored terrorism and illegal arms sales. Worse, 80 percent of Iran's oil reserves were discovered decades ago, with new strikes requiring expensive equipment upgrades that only Russia is offering to underwrite. Having outgrown its frugal innovation and "knowledge-based" development, basic research innovation is frozen due to international sanctions and insular governance. Put simply, the Islamic regime is facing growing domestic unrest and demands for more progress that it simply can't deliver.

What Iran can deliver are cutting-edge drones, based on Western technologies stolen and copied a decade ago, including its Shahed systems and "uncrewed aerial vehicles." Iran's drone program has expanded rapidly from its infancy at the start of the Syrian civil war and has proven highly effective in Russia's invasion of Ukraine.

Then there are the illegal arms. On December 20, 2021, the US Navy seized 1,400 AK-47 assault rifles and a quarter-million rounds of ammunition from an Iranian ship intended for war-torn Yemen; only one month earlier, the Global Initiative Against Transnational Organized Crime announced that over thirteen locations in Somalia had Iranian weapons and ammunition that had been illegally transported to insurgents, also via Yemen. These reports and actual seizures of illegal arms pale in comparison to Iran's support of its Syrian ally. Bashar al-Assad, during his civil war, ongoing since 2011, which has cost over three hundred thousand lives.

And then there's Iran's nuclear program, its distinct troubles in developing it, and its first cyberweapon attack.

The regime seemed hell-bent on having nuclear weapons by 2010. Much like North Korea, Iran mixed frugal innovation with clandestine operations to steal and acquire designs and equipment. Iran was on the verge of enriching uranium; dangerous not just for the world (especially its sworn enemy Israel), but also domestically, as these weren't ideal nuclear facilities. Nor was this the fumbling, and perhaps propagandized, nuclear program of Saddam Hussein's Iraq, which necessitated America's invasion in 2003, bringing his downfall. Iran was a semideveloped and highly militarized nation with the goal of gaining the ultimate weapon through any means.

So the United States, certainly aided by Israel, launched what is known as the world's first cyberweapon: Stuxnet. Due to Iran's inability to manufacture its own full-scale nuclear enrichment facilities, it sourced items worldwide, mostly from black markets. And that was its weakness. Iran used rather basic Microsoft software, and programmable logic controllers (PLCs) made by Siemens, unknowingly creating vulnerabilities at their secret facilities. The centrifuges used to enrich the uranium were the target when the Stuxnet virus was launched sometime in 2009. Intelligently designed to scan and find weaknesses in software and equipment, this "worm" virus finally took control of the PLCs. Centrifuges spin incredibly fast to separate uranium gasses, but Stuxnet was an advanced and rather patient virus, spinning the equipment too fast, then slowing to avoid detection. The centrifuges were soon damaged beyond repair and Iran's enrichment program was compromised. In the end, Iran had no idea what hit them, and the extent of the "first cyberweapon" wasn't fully understood until 2011. Mission accomplished, for now.

Iran still harbored nuclear ambitions, though, so the world negotiated with its leaders for a mutually acceptable compromise. Signed in 2015, the Joint

Comprehensive Plan of Action (JCPOA) brought Iran, the United Kingdom, France, China, Russia, and the United States to the table, allowing Iran to enrich uranium only to levels that can power nuclear plants or for medical experimentation. Since 90 percent enrichment is required for nuclear weapons, the agreed-upon levels (below a maximum of 20 percent) were a major sacrifice for Iran and would be closely monitored by the International Atomic Energy Agency. What the regime received in return was incredibly valuable: several trade sanctions were lifted, Iran was no longer deemed a "rogue state," and seized money totaling around $50 billion was returned, which the regime sorely needed.

This was a breakthrough, but it only lasted three years. In 2018, newly elected US President Donald Trump immediately voided the JCPOA, citing unfounded enrichment activities by Iran. The result was disastrous, and the regime soon restarted its nuclear programs, free from any international inspections, and is now known to be working with North Korea to advance both rogue nations' nuclear aims. It may be too late to put the nuclear genie back in the bottle in Iran.

Then another announcement, in May 2023, further shocked the world: Iran and Saudi Arabia were setting aside years of hostility to move toward peace and closer relations. Even more remarkable was the fact that China brokered the deal. While the differing types of Islam practiced in the two countries was always the great divider (Iran is Shia, Saudi Arabia is Sunni) and a cause for conflict, China had found a mutually beneficial factor—trade—to bring the two nations together.

Could this be a new paradigm? Possibly, although as outlined by the Atlantic Council, "this is neither the end of an era nor the start of one." The formal resumption of diplomatic relations between Iran and Saudi Arabia does not automatically entail or imply any shared innovation and technological exchanges, as occurs within the EU and organizations such as NATO; if anything, it shows how digital and technological evolution has altered the influence variables in the new geopolitical landscape. No longer is it as simple as formally aligning with powerful neighbors and actors; today, one must become actively involved in and part of the innovation ecosystem. So, despite thawing relations with Iran, even Saudi Arabia will not have much interest in sharing technological advancements . . . for now, at least.

Iran's unique status and future have yet to be determined. Expelled from the modern and technological global innovation ecosystem of the West for decades, Iran has achieved a level of innovation (frugal, basic research, and disruptive via drones, but lacking breakthroughs and being unsustainable) as well as proven military strength that now attracts new allies. International credibility is one thing that the regime longs for, as threats have gotten Iran only so far. Stolen, then copied, technologies have bolstered its military and nuclear goals, but there's always something lacking in an insular country with grandiose international ambitions.

Take Iran's announcement in 2023 that the Imam Khomeini University of Marine Sciences and Technologies, in tandem with the Islamic Republican Army, had developed "the first product of quantum processing algorithm." Photos released by the regime showed an impressive computer processor, held by smiling Iranian scientists and military leaders, and the news spread quickly that the rogue state had made a major leap into the future. But Iran's proud new "quantum processor" was just a standard dual-core processor available on Amazon for $599. The international embarrassment quickly went viral. So much for this major innovation by the regime.

What this faux pas highlights is the key issue with the emerging technological gaps on the geopolitical stage. There is only so much a country can accomplish with frugal or stolen innovation, whether it's by willful choice, like North Korea, or through expulsion, like Iran. Gaining foreign technologies via theft, copying, or illegal importation means you will always be trying to get in the game but, ultimately, be found lacking. A nation that's not exposed to the global innovation ecosystem will simply not know what it lacks, with no external feedback to inform it.

Iran faces perhaps its greatest weakness domestically: distrust and growing protests among its vast population of young people. A coup or civil war in Iran is highly possible—its shah was toppled in 1953 by the West, then another in 1978—which would send this emerging nuclear power into chaos. More sanctions won't solve the Iran problem, and suspect allies certainly will only feed increased control by the clerics over the people. The only hope may be for greater openness and, if tenable, more interaction and diplomacy with the West. This won't be easy, given serious suspicions on both sides.

"Death to Israel" has been the rallying cry in Iran for decades. With its unknown advances in its nuclear program, this mantra has become more likely to become a reality. The power of any authoritarian regime is its longevity, outlasting American and other democratically elected leaders, their policies included. Iran did agree to freeze its nuclear program and have it inspected, and then an election far away changed leaders and policies, with "ironclad" international agreements erased in only days. Dictators are also toppled quickly, a sudden spark leading to overthrow, like Muammar Gaddafi in Libya in 2011. Still, the Middle East, and the rest of the world, cannot afford to call Iran's bluff, as its innovations on the battlefield are now tested and proven.

Iran, like North Korea, is struggling with the exponential evolution of innovation, making it difficult for them to keep pace and remain relevant except on the battlefield. Frugal innovation and international theft have brought both only so far, yet domestic unrest and foreign sanctions are dramatically raising the risks. We now must place our trust in diplomacy and the influence of

Iran's allies—rogue and new—to contain and, ideally, help develop peaceful relations. We are at the precipice with Iran, and all must work to avoid catastrophe, regionally and globally.

BIBLIOGRAPHY

BBC News. "Iran Profile—Timeline." January 6, 2020. https://www.bbc.com/news/world-middle-east-14542438.

Esfandiari, Sahar. "These Photos Show What It's Really Like in Iran, Where—Despite Its Antagonistic Relationship with the US—Life Is Surprisingly Normal." *Business Insider*, December 4, 2019. https://www.businessinsider.com/iran-photos-everyday-life-food-shopping-music-sanctions-2019-8#many-iranians-enjoy-going-to-the-mall.

Houreld, Katharine. "Iranian-Supplied Arms Smuggled from Yemen into Somalia." *Reuters*, November 10, 2021. https://www.reuters.com/world/iranian-supplied-arms-smuggled-yemen-into-somalia-study-says-2021-11-10/.

Mazarr, Michael J. "How We Can Keep Iran from Becoming the Next North Korea." RAND Corporation, August 22, 2017. https://www.rand.org/blog/2017/08/how-we-can-keep-iran-from-becoming-the-next-north-korea.html.

Middle East Eye. "Russia to Modernise Iran's Outdated Oil and Gas Industry." May 18, 2023. https://www.middleeasteye.net/news/iran-russia-modernise-dated-oil-gas-industry-press-review.

Office of the High Commissioner for Human Rights. "Behind the Data: Recording Civilian Casualties in Syria." May 11, 2023. https://www.ohchr.org/en/stories/2023/05/behind-data-recording-civilian-casualties-syria#:~:text=In%20the%20ten%20years%20of,of%20civilians%20during%20active%20hostilities.

Robinson, Kali. "What Is the Iran Nuclear Deal?" Council on Foreign Relations, October 27, 2023. https://www.cfr.org/backgrounder/what-iran-nuclear-deal.

Shuster, Mike. "Inside the United States' Secret Sabotage of Iran." *NPR*, May 9, 2011. https://www.npr.org/2011/05/09/135854490/inside-the-united-states-secret-sabotage-of-iran.

United Nations Conference on Trade and Development. "Science, Technology and Innovation Policy Review: The Islamic Republic of Iran." February 2005. https://unctad.org/system/files/official-document/iteipc20057_en.pdf.

United Nations Educational, Scientific and Cultural Organization. "Iran." *UNESCO Science Report 2021*. https://www.unesco.org/reports/science/2021/en/iran?TSPD_101_R0=080713870fab20009fe7cb6c91310b2273dfe7b3d195205e944aeaf700e1608aeb2cfd21edbfc70908937d750f1430000c3ff467873c89c26f1fe6cc5eaec52059f266092297f475c6f5eae69730398224978e519822e5abcc7d359aa4dc3553.

US Department of State. "Illegal Iranian Flow of Weapons to Yemen." December 23, 2021. https://www.state.gov/illegal-iranian-flow-of-weapons-to-yemen/.

Wickens, Katie. "Iran's 'Quantum Processor' Turned Out to Be a $600 Dev Board." *PC Gamer*, June 12, 2023. https://www.pcgamer.com/irans-quantum-processor-turned-out-to-be-a-dollar600-dev-board/.

6

Nigeria, Ethiopia, and South Africa
Struggling to Not Be a Have-Not

Despite living on a continent with chronic poor governance, corruption, inadequate health care and education, civil war, and the plundering of natural resources, Africans are consistently the most optimistic people on Earth. This doesn't mean that they are happy; the 2022 World Happiness Report showed most African people are suffering from a "happiness deficit." Ironically, a 2023 Gallup poll also found that most Africans, especially those under twenty-five years of age, are incredibly hopeful for the future and see progress being made. What these contradictory reports highlight is Africans' universal resilience and belief that things can't get worse, and tomorrow might be better.

Belonging to the global innovation ecosystem, which fosters mutual progress, is critical for rapid modernization. Yet multiple African nations still struggle for varied reasons that must be better understood. As they struggle, others take advantage of Africans with broken promises, resources stolen and sent afar, and puppet rulers who ignore the people. This is the regrettable history of Africa being repeated.

Bones and drawings discovered in the Rising Star cave system in South Africa have revealed the "small-brained" species *Homo naledi*, a people one-third our modern human size yet capable of remarkably creative undertakings. The Rising Star cave system is cramped and treacherous, hundreds of meters deep with miles of interconnected caves. Yet it was here, some three hundred thousand years ago, that these ancient humans made art and buried their dead, a fact that has rewritten our accepted history. The oldest known cave art by *Homo sapiens* or Neanderthals is eighty thousand years old; *Homo naledi* were drawing intricate symbols and pictures almost a quarter million years earlier.

Africa is ancient. Some believe this is a problem, the reason its people are so steadfast in continuing the "old ways" while struggling to advance technologically. This isn't a racial or cultural theory, just a reality. Africa was incredibly advanced; the first white explorers who saw the amazing ruins of Great Zimbabwe simply couldn't believe that the local Africans had built them. Ethiopia's religious and cultural learnings remain so strongly tied to ancient Hebrew teachings that the two must have once enjoyed extensive trade and societal interconnections. Then centuries of European domination stole resources, enslaved populaces, and led to a lack of leadership, decimating Africa's future potential.

In this chapter we focus on three African countries—Nigeria, Ethiopia, and South Africa—to identify how they may overcome inherent and previously external (but now internal) obstacles to become highly innovative. To establish the status of these three countries, let's look to the 2023 Global Innovation Index (see appendix A), published by the World Intellectual Property Organization: Switzerland is ranked number 1 (again), the United States is 3, China is 12, and so on. Way down the rankings, South Africa is 59, Nigeria is 109, and Ethiopia is 125. Based on these rankings alone, all three countries have a long way to go.

Former Nigerian President Goodluck Jonathan knows the time to innovate is now, and has said, "Nowhere in this world now can you move your economy without science and technology. For the next four years we will emphasize so much on S&T because we have no choice; without that we are just dreaming."

Boasting the largest population in all of Africa (over two hundred million), Nigeria is also the continent's biggest oil producer, with the eleventh-largest oil reserves in the world, nearly equal to those of the United States and Libya. Yet, even with this guaranteed source of revenue, its leaders are only now looking to technology to diversify and improve living conditions for their people. Stagnant innovation has been the status quo in Nigeria for years, with a lack of electricity and internet connectivity hampering any high-tech aspirations.

The "curse of crude" hasn't helped Nigeria either, as many oil-rich countries fall behind in all areas other than drilling. For example, Saudi Arabia, once comfortable with its status as a valuable exporter ever in demand, lazed on its oil wealth for decades, only to awaken upon seeing the need to diversify its economy. Nigeria's unique location, as well as its dense population, attracted great attention from major oil and refining leaders, agriculture developers, and even pharmaceutical companies, all begging to be part of its boom. But the boom only happened in the oil sector.

The "curse of crude" is real, and has plagued many countries. Vast oil reserves mean quick cash, while developing other industries, like agriculture and pharmaceuticals, take time. Add government corruption and domestic instability, and you soon have a failed state.

Despite constant demand for its oil, Nigerian government funding remains a struggle, with investment into research and development totaling barely 1 percent of the country's $1 trillion GDP. In 2022, Google spent forty times that amount on R&D. Predictably, and strategically, China has stepped in under the auspices of its Belt and Road Initiative, developing ports and roads in Nigeria and investing over $1 billion USD in Nigeria alone via its Digital Silk Road initiative. Zhongxing Telecommunications Equipment (ZTE) and Huawei are leading this investment, bringing much-needed broadcast and internet capabilities to Nigeria and the African Union. However, these programs come with strings attached: China offers cheap telecommunications equipment with some serious security gaps, not to mention interconnection with a distant, foreign power. Nigeria (despite its oil wealth) is in no position to refuse any aid from outsiders.

Agriculture has always been ripe for innovation in Nigeria and was once a focus. Today, Nigeria imports bananas, which typifies how undeveloped this sector remains. Herein lies another problem that's held true across Africa for far too long: many talented people leave and don't return. According to the US Census Bureau in 2022, Nigerian students are among the best educated. But these Nigerian students are in the United States, having emigrated. This is a huge problem for Nigeria, as many of its most motivated and intelligent people are leaving. Nigeria's second biggest export, after oil, is its people. This is rather bleak, especially compared to Israel's focus on immigrants and developing their skills. Innovation is impossible without talent and government investment.

Nigeria's slow development has led to serious domestic problems. Bridging the old and the new causes conflict, with recurring property and farmer–herder disputes leading to violence. Gang wars and a growing Islamic insurgency also undermine both civilian security and international confidence in investing in Nigeria. In 2021, a *Foreign Affairs* study of Nigeria presented a very stark picture of the country's future: "If a state's first obligation is to provide security and maintain a monopoly on the use of violence, then Nigeria has failed, even if some other aspects of the state still function."

In the early 2000s, there was a meme about a "Nigerian prince" who emailed strangers with a promise of wealth if the recipient would just send a small fee (a scam that netted $150 million in the United Kingdom alone). The reality is that this has become a serious online, black-market operation. These scams, led by gangs seeking easily stolen international funds, are feeding domestic unrest in Nigeria. Today it's not just a Nigerian prince emailing for your help, but a stranger posing as a romantic admirer and sending fake photos and long-term correspondence to unwitting victims, resulting in multiple money transfers to help their new "love." Or worse, fake kidnapping scams and blackmail attempts. Creative and highly technical, these scams originating from Nigeria at least give confidence in their ability to adapt and connect.

Again, Nigeria had the world at its doorstep, with massive oil reserves and a young population eager to work and produce. Oil wealth has not spread across Nigeria evenly, however, so now there is mass inequality and desperation. The world fears that this critical African country could fall into civil war, with dramatic implications far beyond the region.

Personally, I will never forget the time I was in Lagos and met a young app developer named Ayo, who was working from a makeshift office in his grandmother's backyard. With limited resources and sporadic internet service, he passionately shared his vision for connecting rural farmers directly to urban markets. I meet similar young people throughout Africa, talented and inspired, and mostly focused on helping their own people to better connect. Whether in the bustling streets of Addis Ababa or the innovation hubs of Johannesburg, I have witnessed a mosaic of resilience, legacy, and forward momentum. It's these encounters that compel me to delve deeper into the stories of Nigeria, Ethiopia, and South Africa as these countries navigate their unique paths in the global innovation ecosystem.

Ethiopia's position is the opposite of Nigeria's. Ethiopia lacks oil and even the most basic resources, rendering international aid essential. Its leaders have turned to technology to connect its people and, amazingly, this country now has one of the fastest-growing economies in the world. The world is witnessing an aggressive ten-year development plan in action, as Ethiopia strives to become an "African beacon of prosperity."

Technology and education are the cornerstones of this development plan, with China taking the lead, and USAID, the UN, and private companies assisting. Remote Ethiopian villages will be connected to enable e-learning; health care, water, and sanitation systems are being reimagined, and overdue democratic reforms enacted. Ethiopia, despite its proud history and strong religious and cultural ties, was a failed state. So the country had to start from scratch, building basic infrastructure and digital upgrades that have shown immediate and real progress. As a result, Ethiopia's GDP has averaged 10 percent annual growth, with billions in new foreign investment.

China's role in Ethiopia's rapid technological development and adaptation cannot be underestimated. As previously mentioned, China's Digital Silk Road initiative offers fiber-optic wiring, cheap equipment, and massive interconnection across overlooked countries; yet any government's reliance on a single foreign superpower raises growing concerns over domestic affairs. Ethiopia is a major hub for China's technical initiatives across Africa, offering faster connections while also leading to greater influence on Ethiopia's leaders. Ethiopia's entire communications system is purposely designed to be centralized, the internet included, with a single on/off switch to be used solely by its leaders. This is supreme control for a supposedly democratic republic, and it raises concerns over exactly how interconnected its new telecommunications systems will be for the average citizen, especially when factoring in the pressure that China can put on its leaders.

In 2019, Ethiopian Prime Minister Abiy Ahmed received the Nobel Peace Prize for brokering improved relations with longtime foe Eritrea. Then, in 2020, Ahmed launched a war against the Tigray people in the north, displacing millions and leaving thousands dead. The two-year civil war was an atrocity, with massacres and intentional starvation. Ethiopia was once more in the throes of chaos, its rapid technological evolution put on hold, and international aid organizations had to come and save millions of lives. Brief moments of peace and progress are eclipsed by the sparking of more conflict, so Ethiopia's impressive progress hinges on improved leadership and all its people benefiting accordingly.

Few have done more for Africa and Ethiopia than business magnate and philanthropist Bill Gates. In 2022, the Bill and Melinda Gates Foundation pledged $7 billion to bring more health care and sustainable food production to the continent (and that's on top of $9 billion already invested). Gates is focused on the ingenuity of the African people, determined to unleash the potential of its young population, explaining, "Demographically, Africa is the world's youngest continent, and its youth can be the source of a special dynamism. In the next thirty-five years, two billion babies will be born in Africa. By 2050, 40 percent of the entire world's children will live on this continent."

Bill Gates has been especially focused on South Africa for its tech future: "The African entrepreneurs driving start-up booms in the Silicon Savannahs from Johannesburg and Cape Town to Lago and Nairobi are just as young—in chronological age, but also in outlook. The thousands of businesses they're creating are already changing daily life across the continent." The Gates Foundation's successful polio eradication program in Nigeria shows that he is more often right than wrong.

Ethiopia could also benefit from the prescience of Bill Gates; it is only now experiencing modern infrastructure and technology. This comes mostly courtesy of China, with strict centralized controls and 35 percent of its population still living in extreme poverty. Meanwhile, South Africa is considered an "innovation follower." Infrastructure is lacking; so too is investment. A 2016 International Business Report revealed that two-thirds of South African businesses felt disruption and innovation would have "little or no impact on their operations." Worse, 18 percent of South African business executives said they were "not taking any steps to address" disruptive innovation, while 35 percent thought it "would not be applicable" to their business.

This mindset doesn't exactly inspire confidence or change. Like Nigeria, South Africa had every opportunity not too long ago. The world's first heart transplant was performed in Cape Town in 1967, and the CAT scan was also developed in Cape Town. Oil from coal processing was invented in South Africa and still provides 40 percent of the country's fuel. This was once a country on the forefront of multiple technological sectors, a leader in several industries, with a new dawn rising as apartheid ended in 1994. Nelson Mandela was free to lead his nation forward; international aid flowed freely, as did private investment, and many strategic partners were eager to assist.

What happened? The answer is simple: a single political party took control. The African National Congress (ANC) now dominates the South African elections: R&D spending has declined, GDP growth has stagnated, foreign investors became reluctant to invest, and the people have suffered. Despite good universities and networks of entrepreneurs, innovation is hindered by high trade costs and a poor business environment. Most financing is done through loans from family members, with companies' growth limited by a lack of second- or third-stage funding to expand and succeed. Lastly, there is the universal problem of a lack of technical talent, with too many South Africans emigrating abroad for greater opportunities.

Aggressive immigration programs are a recurring theme in all of my work abroad, and certainly key to attracting foreign talent to South Africa, as well as other nations. Still, it must be restated that South Africa once had this talent, only to have it stymied, squandered, and forced to leave. This is a country that had basic research and breakthrough innovation but did not sustain it. So, in mere decades, South Africa devolved to frugal innovation and is mostly dependent on foreign aid. A true innovation ecosystem is required, with better governance, immigration reforms, adequate R&D, and state and private funding. These pillars, independently and combined, are critical.

Corruption is also a major roadblock to development. South Africa's former president, Jacob Zuma, along with his son and other codefendants, were charged in 2021 with multiple bribery and kickback schemes, ranging from milk farms to billion-dollar arms deals. Zuma ignored the corruption inquiry and was sentenced to fifteen months in jail. Zuma's successor, Cyril Ramaphosa, has only increased South Africa's ties to China, and continued the worrisome pattern of arms deals. In May 2023, the Russian ship *Lady R* was docked at the Simon's Town Naval Base, and was declared to be transporting military equipment for the Russian government. This ship was already internationally sanctioned, so any ties between Russia and South Africa are a serious international problem. Today, South Africa still refuses to admit to doing any arms deals with Russia. No matter who is president, corruption and the ignoring of international sanctions seem to continue in South Africa.

Poor leadership has plagued the African nations. When you add in oil, military arms, corruption, famine, disease, desperation, and foreign countries and companies eager to take advantage, it's easy to see why so many African countries struggle. Decades of dependence on international aid has hindered the entrepreneurial instincts of a people who want to be educated, inspired, and then allowed to create for themselves. Just imagine arriving in Silicon Valley replete with unlimited cash, funding each start-up with no accountability, no tracking, no clear deliverables, and no governance or feedback. The system would collapse, and no one would be the wiser. This is the sorry state of the African continent, where charities, private individuals, and nongovernmental organizations race from emergency to emergency but rarely take the time for a full inventory of their impact and progress. For all the good they do in times of emergency, philanthropies and charities are temporary; they cannot replace good government, public and private funding, or R&D. South Africa and Nigeria need collaboration, trade, and immigration, especially by former citizens with a reason to return home with their talents and skills.

The world simply cannot afford more failed states or emergency aid without a wider implementation plan. The creation of an ecosystem in Africa is essential to reignite true innovation. Nations must identify their strengths and weaknesses, such as a young population seeking progress or a lack of universities and funding. Companies can carry much of the weight, with training, initiatives, and employment, but these must be "open" versus closed; China's Digital Silk Road is highly proprietary and serves only China. And, finally, governments must be functional; graft and corruption are poison to any ecosystem. Then the people take over: entrepreneurs focused on using innovation to solve their shared problems, ideas freely flowing, advancements embraced on a level playing field. A thriving global innovation ecosystem depends on hundreds of far smaller satellites feeding the greater coalition. The leap from frugal to basic research, or disruptive to breakthrough innovation, and finally to sustaining, can be remarkable and rapid.

Nigeria's oil won't last forever, and growing domestic unrest undermines its recent government mandate to focus on science and technology, especially with such meager investments in R&D. Ethiopia may indeed become an African beacon of prosperity, but it will take time, and the country faces its own domestic insurgency, serious natural resource limitations, and concerns over the growing influence of China. Meanwhile, South Africa struggles with a lack of honest leadership and the loss of talent.

What could herald a new era in the African nations hinges on unleashing the aspirations of its people. Tying its fortunes to the worldwide strategic initiatives of China is shortsighted, as Africa must rely on proven ecosystems for innovation and development to build its own. Multinationals have already identified several products for Africa to focus on, including a simple cell phone that can be easily manufactured for use by the masses; mobile banking applications for Africa's booming population; even beer based on sorghum or cassava rather than malted barley to reduce shipping, packaging, and other importation costs. Africa could also capitalize on the hard work and investments made by charities and nonprofits by developing and manufacturing more efficient solar arrays, water-well pumping and sanitation systems, or mosquito netting and medicine. These African-made products will save African lives, offer local jobs, and create innovation ecosystems that will only grow.

Conveniently enough, artificial intelligence has emerged as a hyper-efficient path forward, both for Africa and other nations that presently find themselves struggling to join the global innovation ecosystem. Open source AI creates an immediate jump-start for those trying to bridge the gap between present technological limitations and future ambitions. The *2022 State of AI in Africa* report clearly shows which countries are focused on artificial intelligence to reinvent their economies, close economic disparities, and become more competitive. Both South Africa and Nigeria lead Africa's pursuit of artificial intelligence, with 726 and 456 companies that "specialize in AI" in each country, respectively.

As noted above, South Africa once had the expertise to be a medical and biotechnology leader. Via open source AI, there is now a path to rapid return to leadership in this area. While the country's universities and manufacturing facilities remain, South Africa's brain drain must be addressed to foster a future based on basic research and disruptive, even sustaining, innovation. Specifically, immigration must become the focus, with an emphasis on encouraging the talent that left Nigeria and South Africa for greener pastures to finally return. Much like Israel decades ago, the future of both countries hinge on attracting both technical talent and investment from abroad (corporate and government institutions) so that AI can pave a speedy path to catch up to—then eclipse—global players in next-generation medicines and biotechnology.

Nigeria also shows much promise, but with agriculture as its focus. Diversifying from its dependence on oil revenues is paramount, as Nigeria (like South Africa) looks to its past to find its future. Once a major banana exporter (but now importer), a lack of government leadership and a dysfunctional oil-based economy have stymied the economy and failed its people. Today, AI could show Nigerian farmers how, where, and what to plant, as well as which foreign markets are demanding specific agricultural products at any moment. Imagine the impact of AI to better predict how a coming drought or overly wet season will affect regional and global crop yields! Nigeria could rush ahead of the curve, attracting major agribusiness leaders while learning and growing on its own, offering needed employment for its population and becoming the "breadbasket" of Africa. Of course, AI will also have broad implications for oil-producing nations like Nigeria, but those reserves and their revenues must be invested into other sectors, helping Nigeria create a more sustainable, equitable, and prosperous economy, with the bonus of quelling domestic unrest.

Despite its impressive record of economic growth, Ethiopia presents a troubling problem in the AI arena. The country lags far behind South Africa and Nigeria, with only eighteen companies that specialize in the AI sector. This is partly due to the country's economy over the past ten years and simply trying to interconnect and catch up, but it's mostly due to its dependence on China for digital infrastructure and advancements. As a key hub for China's Digital Silk Road, Ethiopia has benefited from new digital infrastructure and its people enjoy upgraded educational, medical, and telecommunications technologies. But there's always the catch-22 of China's Digital Silk Road: nations want it, but they never own it. By allowing China to handle its digital infrastructure, are Ethiopians learning how to do it themselves? How will they become true innovators?

As other nations develop AI tools focused on their country's specific needs and goals, those attached to China via its Digital Silk Road initiative will become even more dependent, and thus more vulnerable to corporate espionage, surveillance, and the threat of being shut down should they not abide by China's foreign policies. China's own secret AI advances and long-term goals simply will not be shared with its many Digital Silk Road beneficiaries. Private companies working in China's AI arena are subjected to strict monitoring or even outright control by the Chinese government, making it incredibly hard for a country to develop an AI strategy while under the same strict controls as Chinese companies. This is the impossible quandary for Ethiopia: the country has advanced rapidly in the past decade, but still faces a quantum leap that its key ally might not permit.

For South Africa, Nigeria, and Ethiopia, the future has never been more promising, nor more uncertain. South Africa can lean on its proud history of critical medical and biotech breakthroughs to use AI to propel itself forward, easing its entry into the global innovation ecosystem. Nigeria can invest its oil wealth into its abundant but neglected agriculture industries to diversify and offer greater stability to its economy and its people. Ethiopia faces the most critical of decisions: fully cede its domestic authority to China (best exemplified by its foreign partner building a "shut-off" switch into Ethiopia's entire digital network to control communications, thus its people), or retain its ability to create its own future. Its leaders may enjoy full control over their people but the risks of being so reliant on a foreign nation, and ending its attachment to China's Digital Silk Road, comes with great risks. But it still isn't too late.

As the continent that will soon bear the majority of the world's population, Africa must look to its ancient past as a world leader and trader to blaze a new future for itself, guided by itself. All of the ingredients are there for this critical continent to choose its own destiny. This is the moment for all African nations, even as the notion of nation-states fades and is slowly replaced by international initiatives and corporations. Such choices have massive implications for all, yet the promise of AI is not forever. The gap between the haves and have-nots will only grow exponentially with the advent of AI, so the world will be watching as Africa works to invent an entirely new future.

It soon may have no choice.

BIBLIOGRAPHY

AI Media Group South Africa. *2002 State of AI in Africa.* AI Media, 2002. https://aiafricareport.gumroad.com/.

Bardien, Ridwaan. "5 Questions Answered about South African Innovation." LinkedIn, March 13, 2017. https://www.linkedin.com/pulse/5-questions-answered-south-african-innovation-ridwaan-bardien/?trk=portfolio_article-card_title.

Campbell, John, and Robert I. Rotberg. "The Giant of Africa Is Failing." *Foreign Affairs*, May 31, 2021. https://www.foreignaffairs.com/articles/africa/2021-05-31/giant-africa-failing.

Christian Science Monitor. "Gallup: 14 of the 15 Most 'Optimistic' Countries Are in Africa. Why?" November 25, 2013. https://www.csmonitor.com/World/Africa/Africa-Monitor/2013/1125/Gallup-14-of-the-15-most-optimistic-countries-are-in-Africa.-Why.

Dahir, Abdi Latif. "Some of the World's Most Unhappy Countries Are Also the Most Optimistic." *Quartz*, March 27, 2017. https://qz.com/africa/942184/some-of-the-worlds-most-unhappy-countries-are-also-the-most-optimistic.

The Economist. "The Zondo Commission Has Revealed Vast Graft in South Africa." June 23, 2022. https://www.economist.com/middle-east-and-africa/2022/06/23/the-zondo-commission-has-revealed-vast-graft-in-south-africa.

Moghalu, Kingsley Chiedu. "Why Has Africa Fallen Behind the Rest of the World's Economies?" *The Guardian*, August 4, 2014. https://www.theguardian.com/global-development/2014/aug/04/africa-fallen-behind-economies-science-technology.

The Nation. "Technology and Innovation in Nigeria: Trends, Challenges, and Opportunities." March 18, 2023. https://thenationonlineng.net/technology-and-innovation-in-nigeria-trends-challenges-and-opportunities/#.

Nextier. "2022 Annual Review of Nigeria's Violent Conflict Profile." April 21, 2023. https://thenextier.com/2022-annual-review-of-nigerias-violent-conflict-situation/ https://www.foreignaffairs.com/articles/africa/2021-05-31/giant-africa-failing.

Ngila, Faustine. "Africa Is Joining the Global AI Revolution." *Quartz*, June 23, 2022. https://qz.com/africa/2180864/africa-does-not-want-to-be-left-behind-in-the-ai-revolution.

Shapshak, Toby. "Bill Gates on Africa: Tomorrow's Innovations Depend on Today's Opportunities for Youth." *Forbes*, July 17, 2016. https://www.forbes.com/sites/tobyshapshak/2016/07/17/bill-gates-on-africa-tomorrows-innovations-depend-on-todays-opportunities-for-youth/?sh=1b026dce7b95.

United Nations Conference on Trade and Development. "How to Launch Ethiopia's Tech and Innovation Lift-Off." November 19, 2019. https://unctad.org/news/how-launch-ethiopias-tech-and-innovation-lift.

Wong, Kate. "This Small-Brained Human Species May Have Buried Its Dead, Controlled Fire and Made Art." *Scientific American*, June 5, 2023. https://www.scientificamerican.com/article/this-small-brained-human-species-may-have-buried-its-dead-controlled-fire-and-made-art/.

World Bank. "South Africa Economic Update: More Innovation Could Improve Productivity, Create Jobs, and Reduce Poverty." September 2017. https://www.worldbank.org/en/country/southafrica/publication/south-africa-economic-update-more-innovation-could-improve-productivity-create-jobs-and-reduce-poverty.

World Economics. "Nigeria's Gross Domestic Product." 2022. https://www.worldeconomics.com/Country-Size/Nigeria.aspx.

Part III

THE BENEFITS AND FEARS OF BEING INSIDE

7

The United States, China, and India

Moonshots

There are moments in history of such paramount importance that we can later point to them and say, "Here. This was when everything changed."

The "fire lance" first entered the battlefield in the early twelfth century: bamboo tubes that could shoot flames, later packed with debris to violently project shards of pottery and pellets at the enemy. The first known gun, based on centuries of Chinese experimentation with black powder, forever altered warfare and rendered expensive armor, a millennia of accepted military strategies, and even the sword extinct. Around 4000 BCE, the invention of the wheel brought the wagon and chariot, facilitating the transport of people and goods, along with communications and trade. In May 1776, English physician Edward Jenner injected pus from cowpox blisters into a young boy, giving the first vaccination and marking the beginning of the end of nearly three thousand years of smallpox epidemics worldwide.

We are at another moment paramount to history.

An actual moonshot is underway, although some may be too isolated to take part in or benefit from it. While some countries have purposely sealed themselves off from the outside world (North Korea), and others have been sealed off due to their toxic behavior (Iran), many more (South Africa and Nigeria) struggle to gain access to the global innovation ecosystem that fosters true change and development. For those who collaborate, though, the future is now.

Governments, universities, corporations, and individuals who are free to share ideas and technology are seeing results that are impossible to fully grasp. The Human Genome Project, boldly announced in 2003, became an international effort to determine the base pairs and sequencing of human DNA. It's been comparatively inexpensive, at $2.7 billion over thirteen years, and we now understand inherited diseases, cancer risks, and possible cures. With a simple at-home swab test, you can learn your entire genetic lineage within days. The same technology is also helping to solve long-forgotten crimes by matching murderers' DNA with "cold case" evidence. Few in 2003 could imagine all we'd have learned from this one project in only twenty years.

This is shared technological progress witnessed in real time. With our massive computing power, soon to be supercharged by the promise of quantum computing and artificial intelligence, our capacity to fully understand and solve the world's problems is literally at our fingertips.

One of those problems: cancer. The disease kills over six hundred thousand people and costs a quarter of a trillion dollars annually in America alone. Announced in 2016, the Cancer Moonshot initiative is a commonsense investment that easily pays for itself, with around $2 billion budgeted annually by the White House to cure cancer by 2050. Worldwide, cancer is estimated to kill nearly twenty million people annually by 2030, and cost the world $25 trillion total by 2050, which means the Cancer Moonshot initiative is as essential as it is invaluable. Now consider the impact of dementia and Alzheimer's disease, which affect over fifty-five million people worldwide and cost nearly $2 trillion each year. The Human Genome Project is already paying dividends in helping us understand Alzheimer's, so another moonshot initiative with a remarkable return on investment will soon be a reality.

Currently, our major limitation is the human brain's ability to absorb information fast. We are slowed by our fingers typing on keyboards, and voice commands aren't much faster. Elon Musk's Neuralink brain implant, which is just one of many exciting initiatives in this area, seeks to solve this issue by implanting a small chip in the human brain to dramatically increase our ability to upload information, commands, and experiences to a computer. Instead of waiting for a single web page to load, users will be downloading and uploading entire movies in seconds, but the movies will be our commands and memories. The military is excited about this major innovation, as are doctors who can use this technology to repair traumatic brain injuries and help stroke survivors.

As the military and neurotechnology become more entwined, dual-use technologies have also proven efficient and cost-effective. For every brain implant developed to "cure" Parkinson's or Alzheimer's, there is a scientist who will see the potential to use that technology to create a super-soldier. Is this a mixed blessing? Soldiers injured in battle could also benefit from the same tech they deploy. A soldier with brain damage, or a stroke victim, can both be neurologically retrained with new technologies that parrot a mirror image of basic functions, such as grabbing a glass of water. With repeated therapy, the human brain has shown the ability to rewire itself while "watching" a mirror image of the good arm repeatedly performing tasks, slowly "tricking" the brain so the disabled arm will function properly again. Isn't that amazing?

In the end, this is all about health, whether repairing damage from an injury or attack or recovering from sickness and aging. Aging is the new target.

Based on the most recent and readily available data, health care costs average around $80,000 for the average American's final year of life; hospital costs nearly double that to $56,300 in the last three months. Denmark and Germany report slightly lower costs, with an average of $50,000 to $60,000 per patent. Taiwan has reported the lowest end-of-life costs at around $20,000 per patient, while the United Kingdom's limited data shows significantly less spending compared to other developed countries. A recent study on advanced illness and end-of-life care by the global nonprofit Health Affairs (Health Affairs.org) found that governments spend more to ensure elderly people are more comfortable and cared for at the end of their lives, but do not waste money on drastic attempts to unnecessarily prolong those lives. These dollar figures are averages, but what pushes the costs higher—raising budgetary concerns and conspiracy theories of health-care dollars being "wasted"—are patients suffering from chronic illnesses.

The elderly constitute the smallest portion of the world's population, at around 17 percent. However, the costs of caring for the elderly are among the highest, accounting for 37 percent of the total cost of government and personal health care. Critically, it is a small portion of elderly people suffering from chronic illnesses (such as cancer, dementia, and debilitating pain), that are bankrupting the world's health-care budgets. Coupled with lower birth rates worldwide, this means we are facing an untenable future, with fewer workers paying for increasingly expensive health care for older people.

There is a glimmer of hope. America's Cancer Moonshot is already showing progress, and artificial intelligence combined with quantum computing offers extraordinary leaps in health care by quickly analyzing each person's unique DNA, protein, and molecular makeup with the goal of creating "designer" drugs meant to cure their specific disease. We are on the verge of curing our friends, family, and neighbors of cancer, Alzheimer's, Parkinson's, and other chronic diseases that lead to increased health-care spending, while also avoiding bankruptcy.

This is far bigger than spiraling health-care budgets, though. No one wants to feel useless or like a burden on others. Through advanced health-tech that is already being released, we are about to witness a new era for the elderly. As mentioned in the introduction, I lost my father to brain cancer; more than two hundred thousand people worldwide die from this specific disease each year. Since I share this genetic profile with my father, I may suffer his same fate.

We all must remain optimistic. The future is now.

Globally, massive projects are becoming the norm. Horizon 2020 was an $80 billion initiative across the European Union (from 2014 to 2020) to study more sustainable development, climate change solutions, and cross-integration strategies (i.e., innovation ecosystems). Now known as Horizon Europe, the initiative has a budget of $95 billion, deploying pollution abatement in the Mediterranean, new "zero carbon" technologies, scalable innovation, and job training programs across multiple nations. Artificial intelligence and sustainable energy will be major focuses of Horizon Europe, while the theme of shared innovation remains at the forefront. Interestingly, after the United Kingdom left the EU via Brexit, thinking it could work unilaterally, the relevance of Horizon Europe became even more evident, forcing the United Kingdom to rejoin this critical innovation ecosystem.

No nation is an island, and Horizon Europe underscores this new geopolitical reality. While the United States may be a leader in funding and research for its Cancer Moonshot initiative, the greater global innovation ecosystem—one that includes the United States, Canada, European countries, and India, as well as Middle Eastern and Asian allies—is a force as yet unseen.

The largest solar farm in the world is found not in the United States or China, but India. Bhadla Solar Park generates enough clean energy to power 1.3 million homes and avoid the creation of 375,000 tons of carbon dioxide. India has become a critical information technology leader, primarily outsourcing its talent and skills to others. However, this democratic country is now looking inward, unleashing its IT expertise to quickly modernize multiple domestic sectors.

In August 2023, the world took notice when India launched and landed an unmanned rover on the moon. More remarkable was the total cost: $74 million (Russia's failed lunar South Pole moon lander cost $200 million and crashed). Meanwhile, NASA is budgeting well over $433 million for its own Viper rover expedition on the moon. India has leapt from basic research to disruptive and now sustainable innovation, utilizing its domestic expertise to suddenly emerge as a global leader. As China's economy has slowed, showing serious problems as an international exporter, India's economy is booming at over 7 percent GDP growth annually.

The rapid adoption of new technologies like solar can be breathtaking in impact and, at times, a bit embarrassing. For example, Texas is proudly pro oil production and so steadfast in its energy independence that the state's one power grid is intentionally not connected to the rest of the country ("Powered by Texans, for Texans"). Unfortunately, the Lone Star State's grid is also not weatherized, which led to catastrophic blackouts after record-setting storms and a deep freeze during the winter of 2021. And, because it is fully independent of outside sources, it must stand on its own as multiple failures and weaknesses are identified. As a result, Texas has quickly (and quietly) become a mostly unheralded leader in solar and wind farm installations, accounting for one-quarter of all new installations across the United States since 2021. When a "heat dome" covered the state in the summer of 2023, spiking temperatures to well over 100 degrees Fahrenheit, even Texans had to acknowledge that non-oil power supplies (wind and solar, specifically) were keeping its grid and air conditioners running. Citing this success, as well as high natural gas prices, Texas is now making solar a critical part of its energy infrastructure, spending $20 billion over the next five years to produce thirty-six gigawatts, creating over ten thousand jobs and enough power for thirty million homes.

This is how quickly change can occur, whether due to national strategy or in response to a disaster. By participating in the global innovation ecosystem, and having access to the best available talent and technology, even reluctant states like Texas benefit immediately. Saudi Arabia, another major oil producer, announced in 2023 that it is building the largest solar power plant in the world in its Mecca province. To take advantage of its abundance of sunlight and offset the global price swings of oil, the kingdom will invest $40 billion to develop 70 percent of its renewable energy capacity by 2030 and be carbon-neutral by 2050. Such projects and goals are both environmentally responsible and good for national economic security, especially considering China's migration to Russia as its main oil supplier, unseating Saudi Arabia.

More efficient technologies combined with shared expertise are erasing long-held beliefs, allowing for the rapid implementation of alternative methods. This extends far beyond new solar and wind farms. Soft power and strategic influence grow and spread in tandem, as countries and companies long to be part of the global innovation ecosystem and push for change. Few would have dared imagine a Middle East with Saudi Arabia inviting Israel to be part of its NEOM initiative, just as Sunni Muslim Saudi Arabia's shocking truce with Shia Muslim Iran was utterly unexpected—and brokered by China. The geopolitical stakes have never been higher, and the usual norms no longer apply.

Technological standards, compliance, and advancements are the by-products, especially as China's Digital Silk Road spreads around the world, vying to unseat the leadership of the United States. Given new strategic partnerships, some are hopeful (Israel and Saudi Arabia), while others remain dubious (Iran and North Korea; China and Russia), but the critical role of the United States must be noted. China's ascendance has brought American dominance into question, yet the world has never known a leader like the United States.

Since World War II, when the Marshall Plan helped rebuild Europe at a cost of nearly $200 billion in today's dollars, then demilitarized Japan and rebuilt its economy, the United States has transformed from an isolated, reluctant participant in world affairs to one that offered investment and security while encouraging trade. Instead of investing in its military, Japan quickly became a global leader in innovation and exports, as did South Korea and Taiwan as they reformed, then rebuilt, after years of conflict. The international mistakes of the United States are many—the Korean "conflict" and Vietnam, multiple coups in Iran and South America—yet its role has been unique in world history. From military might to digital innovations, including the "invention" of the internet and Silicon Valley's outsized dominance of global technology, the United States was and remains a beacon for freedom and advances. Now, as its leadership is being challenged on the world stage, the very notion of nations is also in question. Global corporations have more power and influence, economically and politically, than ever.

On June 30, 2023, Apple Inc. became the first $3 trillion corporation. This single American company now has a higher net worth than the GDPs of all but five countries: China, Japan, Germany, India and, of course, the United States. Imagine Apple's soft power over suppliers: for example, it employs around three hundred thousand workers at a single Foxconn factory in China to make iPhones. However, its leaders have voiced concerns over parts of its supply chain and may turn to India and Vietnam for future factories. The United States and China may promise favorable trade deals, new physical and digital infrastructure, and other carrots to encourage trade and closer ties with other countries, but Apple brings immediate investment and jobs. This is real soft power unseen on the world's stage, as digital ambassadors from multiple countries vie to influence companies like Apple instead of countries.

Organizationally, the United Nations suffers from an inherent flaw of its Security Council: its five permanent members (the United States, Russia, China, France, and the United Kingdom) rarely agree with each other regarding any major international issue other than the need to avoid a nuclear war. Meanwhile, NATO has served a critical role by countering the former USSR, as well as other rogue states. No single nation can stand alone on the world stage, and NATO's role has only grown as the notion of nation-states comes into question.

Ironically, many of NATO's efforts are rarely known until they fail. This is illustrated by asking a simple question: where is NATO's headquarters? The answer: virtually everywhere. Brussels, Belgium, may be NATO's symbolic and physical headquarters, but an hour and a half south in Mons is NATO's Cyberspace Operations Centre. NATO's Cooperative Cyber Defence Centre of Excellence is found in the most unlikely of places: Tallinn, Estonia. This center is the epitome of digital interconnection. It boasts the active participation of thirty-eight NATO and non-NATO member nations, offering a range of tech expertise, from network security to cyberintelligence, coordination by and for military commanders from multiple countries, research and development, and even education and consultation. The center's critical mission is "lessons learned" from every cyberattack, as intelligence is shared and systems are enhanced. Whatever its critics and enemies may say, NATO has never been more indispensable.

This is the global innovation ecosystem in action: dozens of countries working and learning together, both preventing and coordinating cyberattacks and defenses. While NATO was originally created to counteract Soviet aggression, the rise of China and rogue hackers have become serious threats. At least 650,000 Chinese hackers are known to be active at every minute of every day. The US Federal Bureau of Investigation acknowledged in 2023 that China has fifty hackers for every one FBI agent, meaning that the world's most powerful nation for the past seventy-five years is simply outnumbered. Russia and North Korea's highly skilled hackers, in addition to China's, make NATO's multiple cyberspace and defense centers essential for global security in the digital age. Cybercrimes total hundreds of billions in annual thefts, while critical infrastructure and military sites are regular targets. The stakes have never been higher.

But breakthroughs are happening quickly. While China's Belt and Road and Digital Silk Road initiatives have spread its soft power and trade globally, the focus on standardized China-based technology hampers both national independence and innovation. In July 2023, my birthplace of Italy announced that it sought to void its Belt and Road agreement with China, citing minimal boost to exports after four years and calling its decision to partner with China "improvised and atrocious." Other underdeveloped nations still eagerly accept China's inexpensive infrastructure upgrades, but they become locked into that same technology, with China capable of monitoring communications and potentially turning off "franchises" that don't fully embrace their benefactor's international aims.

Meanwhile, members of the global innovation ecosystem continue to advance through collaboration and lessons learned. This is not a closed system, as exemplified by NATO's cyber center in Estonia, which retains flexibility in a world made more unstable by cyberthreats, the dissolution of nation-states, and the rise of international corporations versus countries.

Pondering the progress underway in the global innovation ecosystem, such as benefits to members and limits to nonmembers, can be mind-boggling. A cure for cancer or Alzheimer's disease are game-changers for millions of people, saving impacted nations trillions of dollars. Now, limit those cures to only member nations, with no one else benefiting. Some are able to save millions of lives and trillions of dollars, while elsewhere, millions die and trillions are wasted. This is the harsh reality of a single breakthrough selectively shared.

One stark example of this was in 2020 as the COVID-19 pandemic spread around the world. Developed nations shared vaccines and testing kits, while outliers attempted to develop their own versions of the vaccine. Russia shocked the medical world by announcing the first "approved" COVID-19 vaccine, which it dubbed Sputnik V. Yet even Russian President Vladimir Putin was reluctant to receive his nation's vaccination, inciting domestic distrust. As a result, Russia's inoculation rates fell far below those of other developed countries. Considered an international public relations stunt rather than an approved and tested vaccine, Sputnik V was the latest tremor in a growing rift between those inside the global innovation ecosystem and those outside of it. China's "zero COVID" policy nearly broke its economy and sparked massive domestic unrest, showing that the consequences of remaining outside the global innovation ecosystem can be dire.

This is a universal fear of those inside the global innovation ecosystem: others falling so far behind that they can't catch up. Or, maybe worse, some won't share their discoveries.

Cures and solutions, whether medical or technical, a vaccination or cyberdefense, are being invented and adopted regularly, and their dissemination between partners is essential. Ask yourself: Would China share quantum computing if they were the first to discover it? What about breakthroughs in artificial intelligence? Those skeptical of American leadership might ask the same questions. It's safe to say that NATO members benefit daily from shared knowledge, whether cyberattacks or military intelligence, yet what's most worrisome are certain countries falling so far behind that they simply could not adopt nor integrate a major leap in technology on the horizon.

Could North Korea's Kim regime embrace or even deploy an American-made cure for cancer? The hatred instilled in all North Koreans toward America stirs too much distrust, which in part explains why statistics for the regime's supposedly successful response to "high fever" (COVID-19) are generally accepted as pure propaganda. Critically, could North Korea's antiquated health-care system and digital infrastructure even handle a major medical or technological innovation that might positively impact its people? Do they have the equipment, software and hardware, never mind the technical expertise? Would the Kim regime allow it, or see it as a threat to its authority?

Iran's youthful population continues to protest for change from the despotic Islamic clerics in power. If clean, infinite nuclear fusion was to be discovered and readied for global deployment, would leaders of oil-rich nations like Iran embrace it? Saudi Arabia has shown a willingness to diversify its cash cow, but could Putin in Russia? Now tied to China through oil exports, Putin's power remains pinned to the price of oil, so any alternatives challenge his position.

I must often remind myself that it's not always the seismic invention that brings real change. I was recently walking through a bustling tech expo in Saudi Arabia when I suddenly remembered a dimly lit workshop in rural

Pakistan. There, a decade ago, a local innovator showed me his prototype of a simple hand-cranked device meant to purify water. Its potential impact on the community was clear, yet resources and recognition eluded him. Fast-forward to the Saudi Arabia expo, where I was surrounded by cutting-edge technology proudly on display: AI-driven solutions, genomics, and sustainable energy marvels. The stark contrast between these two moments underscores the theme of this book: while some make giant leaps in technology and innovation, others strive for a foothold on the ladder of progress. These global moonshots transform societies, but they also spotlight the global disparities in access and opportunities.

We can't overlook the minor inventions, nor their creators, when they are most needed and deserving of notice.

This is another paramount moment in history. Dozens of nations, myriad universities and corporations, are working together to both innovate and defend. Meanwhile, a handful of nations stand isolated to retain their authority. Many advance while others grasp at outdated notions, soon to be obsolete. We now witness these moments in the ruins of time. While some united to share intellectual and military strength, as evidenced by the Greek city-states and the Allied powers during World War II, others were too focused on securing their limited position, hubris proving their weakness. We still cite and praise these victors from our past. Meanwhile, the names of those who failed to change and innovate are forgotten.

Who was the greater inventor, Nikola Tesla or Thomas Edison? Both men used existing discoveries in electricity to envision, then create new products, breakthroughs that benefited all of humanity. Now, consider those who never tried, or failed to adapt. Did they know their time was passing quickly, or that it was already too late?

BIBLIOGRAPHY

Armellini, Alvise. "Italy Minister: Joining China's Belt and Road Was 'Atrocious' Decision." *Reuters*, July 30, 2023. https://www.reuters.com/world/joining-chinas-belt-road-was-an-atrocious-decision-italy-minister-2023-07-30/.

Borowitz, Mariel. "India's Chandrayaan-3 Landed on the South Pole of the Moon—A Space Policy Expert Explains What This Means for India and the Global Race to the Moon." Space.com, September 3, 2023. https://www.space.com/india-chandrayaan-3-global-moon-race.

Bresnahan, Timothy F., and Manuel Trajtenberg. "General Purpose Technologies 'Engines of Growth'?" *Journal of Econometrics* 65, no. 1 (1995): 83–108. https://sciencedirect.com/science/article/pii/030440769401598T.

European Commission. "Horizon 2020." March 15, 2021. https://research-and-innovation.ec.europa.eu/funding/funding-opportunitiesfunding-programmes-and-open-calls/horizon-2020_en.

European Society for Medical Oncology. "Estimate of the Global Economic Cost of the Most Prevalent Cancers in 204 Countries from 2020 to 2050." March 3, 2023. https://www.esmo.org/oncology-news/estimate-of-the-global-economic-cost-of-the-most-prevalent-cancers-in-204-countries-from-2020-to-2050.

French, Eric B., Jeremy McCauley, Maria Aragon, et al. "End-of-Life Medical Spending in Last Twelve Months of Life Is Lower Than Previously Reported." *Health Affairs*, July 2017. https://www.healthaffairs.org/doi/10.1377/hlthaff.2017.0174.

Kennedy, Ryan. "Utility-Scale Updates on Texas 36 GW Five-Year Solar Path." *PV Magazine*, February 3, 2023. https://pv-magazine-usa.com/2023/02/03/utility-scale-updates-on-texas-36-gw-five-year-solar-path/.

Kratzer, Christopher. "The Enigma of the Norden Bombsight." Maxwell Air Force Base, January 20, 2012. https://www.maxwell.af.mil/News/Display/Article/420450/the-enigma-of-the-norden-bombsight/.

Lee, Sook Jong. "Rebuilding the US–South Korea–Japan Trilateral Relations in the Indo-Pacific Region." Wilson Center, May 23, 2022. https://www.wilsoncenter.org/article/rebuilding-us-south-korea-japan-trilateral-relations-indo-pacific-region.

Lockett, Charles J. "The First Guns: How Gunpowder Overcame the Sword." *The Collector*, January 26, 2022. https://www.thecollector.com/first-guns/.

National Library of Medicine. "The Global Burden of Cancer: Priorities for Prevention." January 2010. https://www.ncbi.nlm.nih.gov/pmc/articles/PMC2802672/.

Nelson, Jennifer. "How the Texas Power Grid Works and Why It Failed." *Investopedia*, June 7, 2023. https://www.investopedia.com/texas-power-grid-5207850.

Quick Quote. "The Cost of End of Life Care: 48 Facts for Families and Caregivers." November 15, 2023. https://www.quickquote.com/end-of-life-care-costs-statistics/.

Riedel, Stefan. "Edward Jenner and the History of Smallpox and Vaccination." National Institutes of Health, January 2005. https://www.ncbi.nlm.nih.gov/pmc/articles/PMC1200696/.

Sharwood, Simon. "China Has 50 Hackers for Every FBI Cyber Agent, Says Bureau Boss." *The Register*, May 1, 2023. https://www.theregister.com/2023/05/01/fbi_director_wray_china_testimony/.

Stronski, Paul. "What Went Wrong with Russia's Sputnik V Vaccine Rollout?" Carnegie Endowment for International Peace, November 15, 2021. https://carnegieendowment.org/2021/11/15/what-went-wrong-with-russia-s-sputnik-v-vaccine-rollout-pub-85783.

Toh, Michelle. "Foxconn Has Recruited 100,000 New Workers for Largest iPhone Factory, State Media Reports." CNN, July 18, 2022. https://www.cnn.com/2022/11/18/business/foxconn-recruitment-china-covid-iphone-production-intl-hnk/index.html.

Wimo, Anders, Katrin Seeher, Rodrigo Cataldi, et al. "The Worldwide Costs of Dementia in 2019." *Alzheimer's & Dementia*, January 8, 2023. https://alz-journals.onlinelibrary.wiley.com/doi/10.1002/alz.12901.

8

The World Brain

What Artificial Intelligence Is and Isn't

Thus far, we have highlighted specific countries and international initiatives, and how each is affected by innovation. Various paths have been taken, with varying rates of success. The global innovation ecosystem is now poised to make huge leaps that those who are unengaged or purposely defiant won't be able to benefit from or catch up to. Whether using frugal, basic research, disruptive, breakthrough, or sustaining innovation, the revolution that is artificial intelligence could soon alter all geopolitics, the very notion of nations, and humanity as we know it.

But here's the paradox: a nation with AI may be capable of skipping the many stages of innovation. However, without these stages, AI is unattainable for that same nation. Once the challenges and implications of AI are fully understood, little makes sense. Until, of course, it's too late.

Massively disruptive technologies don't come along often, but when they do, the entire Earth shudders. For over a half century we have enjoyed the benefits of semiconductors, advanced electronics, and GPS. Even space travel has been normalized, all thanks to brilliant minds and collaboration by so many unsung heroes. Moving forward, AI offers us extraordinary opportunities, or possibly abject ruin, depending on whom you ask. Once AI has moved out of its current infancy and its long-term impacts are fully understood, we must control it by providing development standards, international compliance standards, and clear guardrails. The stakes will simply be too high tomorrow.

"Whoever becomes the leader in this sphere will become the ruler of the world." Who said this about artificial intelligence? Sci-fi visionary Isaac Asimov? Mathematician Stephen Hawking? Guess again: Vladimir Putin, in 2017. This was five years before he launched a second, catastrophic, invasion of Ukraine, squandering lives, treasure, and international standing. Russia's calamity in Ukraine has also undermined its essential AI development for the foreseeable future.

What was a major domestic initiative in Russia and deemed essential to regain world power by its leader, became a government mandate in 2020 through the new State Armaments Program (part of the FPI), promising robotic soldiers powered by AI on the ground, in the air, and underwater. Russia spent $4.7 billion rubles ($51 million USD) on AI in 2021, which was enough to attract tech talent and spark university research. Then Russia invaded Ukraine, and funding shifted to its quagmire at the western border. The resulting international sanctions led to the loss of access to semiconductors and related AI technology, and talented researchers soon left Russia for more stable universities and better funding elsewhere. By 2022 (two years after launching its AI initiative), Putin was blaming capital markets rather than his invasion of Ukraine for Russia's flagging AI efforts. Critically, Russia's efforts were highly siloed, meaning they were isolated and developed with little to no outside influence (i.e., an anti-innovation ecosystem). Practical deployment of AI remains in question. Russia now appears to be deferring to China, its newest oil export partner, for AI breakthroughs, a symptom of a failing nation that must rely on others for innovation.

This isn't abnormal when it comes to AI. According to Gartner Research, in 2023, 35 percent of companies were using AI while 42 percent were exploring using AI in the future. There are 195 countries in the world, and they are outnumbered by the tens of thousands of companies that are using, planning to use, or creating AI. Considering the lack of international standards for AI development, such as ethics and compliance, the question is not whether a company is using AI, but which AI it's using. Are there any guardrails or fail-safes? Or have we reached that movie scene where an AI system achieves sentience, goes haywire, and destroys everything?

When ChatGPT exploded onto the scene in November 2022, it was an "artificial intelligence development tool" that caused a frenzy. Microsoft immediately invested in ChatGPT, and Wall Street speculated billions on this latest tech boom, with the result that chip designers like Nvidia reached values of over $1 trillion overnight. And then something odd happened: use of ChatGPT plummeted, dropping over 10 percent in 2023. Was the ChatGPT craze just another moment of internet viral fancy, was it the long-promised revolution, or did other factors play a part?

ChatGPT is censored; sexual and violent content are purposely restricted (based on algorithms), so nothing deemed "harmful, offensive or illegal" is allowed. Some users balked at this limitation. When Microsoft got involved in ChatGPT, even more users were turned off. Predictably, competing uncensored "artificial intelligence tools" quickly appeared, offering more explicit content and grabbing users. Unsurprisingly, the pornography industry has been among the earliest adopters of many technologies, including digital video, internet streaming, paywalls, and now AI. This lack of censorship means that users can now create explicit videos exploiting both public and private photos of celebrities, friends, and enemies. Politicians have followed suit, using AI tools to create fake photos and videos to slander opponents and spread favorable propaganda. Any new invention can quickly be adapted for alternative uses, oftentimes by the most depraved users—pornographers and politicians included.

Despite the hype, what few are publicly saying is how flawed today's artificial intelligence tools truly are. This isn't AI at all; it's Ford's Model T compared to a McLaren Formula 1 race car.

Standard data sets are used to "power" today's concept of artificial intelligence: numeric data (to train applications to identify objects, patterns, or trends), categorical data (to cluster and classify), image data, text data, audio data, sensor data (for behavior and vision), and structured data (databases and spreadsheets). These data sets are what AI "knows."

Any internet search about "artificial intelligence" is what feeds this data; it captures your computer or cell phone's location and browsing history and shares them with myriad, mostly unknown, third parties. Privacy has historically remained a largely ignored argument in internet development. Browser beware.

"Artificial intelligence is only as good as our data." This is the rallying cry of both AI researchers and those who oppose its advancement. Tesla CEO and X CTO Elon Musk has expressed both excitement and concern over AI for years. In July 2023, Musk limited the number of daily tweets any user can read to six hundred (later raised to a thousand) on the platform formerly known as Twitter. His policy, as well as changing the name from Twitter to X, both highlight Musk's ever-evolving ideas, including limiting how AI developers can utilize user data to "learn." Whether it's called "data scraping" or "system manipulation," this is about limiting access to ravenous AI tools that require more data to function better.

"Garbage in, garbage out." That's the mantra for software databases and AI developers. This is already a problem in the AI world. In June 2023, US District Court Judge Kevin Castel sanctioned and fined two lawyers for using ChatGPT to write their legal briefing, resulting in a document so flawed that fictitious cases were cited as legal precedent. When the lawyers asked ChatGPT to write their legal briefing, it invented cases that didn't exist. The two lawyers (however lazily) agreed with the AI tool's results and presented it in court to the rather unimpressed federal judge.

What happened? Was ChatGPT "hallucinating" or inventing content from unknown sources, as some AI researchers have observed? There were no known fake court precedents available as data sets to be fed into a machine learning tool. If the data wasn't flawed (however limited the available data sets may be), was it an inherent flaw in AI? Perhaps it was both. Some experts have noted that the fourth version of ChatGPT is "dumber" than earlier versions. A joint 2023 study by Stanford University and University of California, Berkeley showed lower accuracy and higher biases in the AI tool's results: earlier versions of ChatGPT had a 97.6 percent success rate in identifying prime numbers, while the fourth (and latest) version dropped to a startling 2.4 percent accuracy rate. Unrelated improvements to the ChatGPT tool can affect other, seemingly unrelated, capabilities. Even OpenAI, ChatGPT's parent company, acknowledged that "When you use [ChatGPT] more heavily, you start noticing issues you didn't see before."

It's important to take a step back and truly consider what we are building. This is especially relevant when I am advising clients. Most are enthralled by the potential without being fully aware of its problems. I loathe being the skeptic, but color me unimpressed.

Artificial intelligence tools may be fine for now—interesting tech to play with and maybe create something yet unseen. But they are only tools. What AI presently promises is something entirely different: the ability to cut costs versus preserving jobs. This is why the 2023 writers' strike in Hollywood was so significant: Writers Guild of America members demanded that screenplays not be fed into AI tools, while actors demanded that their likenesses remain real, not virtual. However, Hollywood film producers see an opportunity for massive savings by using AI, cutting scriptwriting costs as well as background actors who no longer need to be hired, but can be created during editing. The settlement of the WGA strike in September 2023 stipulated that AI cannot be credited for writing any films or TV shows, while feeding screenplays into AI remains an ongoing concern.

The film industry isn't alone in its battle over AI. Authors and music artists have sued to prevent their work from being co-opted by AI tools to invent new "art." German photographer Boris Eldagsen sparked a debate about AI and art when he won the prestigious Sony World Photography Award for his entry "Pseudomnesia: The Electrician." Eldagsen rejected the award, announcing that he'd used AI to create his photograph, remarking that he was being a "cheeky monkey."

Again, is this AI? A novelty, or fun tools that show us how the capabilities of computers can unleash our imaginations? Or is AI beyond our capacity to even dream?

DeepMind was founded in Britain in 2010, then acquired by Google in 2014. DeepMind is publicly touted as a "neural network" known mostly for playing video games, winning against professional (and human) go, chess, and shogi players around the world. Is this another quaint novelty? Not even close. DeepMind mimics how human brains work; it uses reinforced learning (playing a game over and over) while also utilizing a unique form of short-term memory to solve specific problems. This has revolutionary implications. Reinforced learning may sound like two participants playing a game, finishing, and then starting over; but DeepMind is forever playing multiple games with multiple players millions of times every second—and learning each time. The average human would need a hundred lifetimes to accomplish what DeepMind has completed in the time it took to read this sentence. Nowhere will DeepMind's impact be felt more deeply than in the handling of the most complex quandary we face: our two hundred million protein structures and how they affect our health, diseases, and ways to treat them.

Welcome to true AI: DeepMind will disrupt the pharmaceutical development of the future. Rather than developing a few drugs after years and years of testing, then approvals or rejections by the US Food and Drug Administration (FDA) or the EU, DeepMind can curate designer drugs for each individual based on their DNA, specific protein structures, and flaws. Much as the Human Genome Project can use a buccal smear to spit out our entire genetic lineage in a few days, DeepMind will take that swab and invent a unique treatment for your cancer, Alzheimer's, diabetes, or other disease, which large pharmaceutical companies simply can't develop, either due to cost or ability.

When considering the next logical step in AI development, most imaginations turn to the military. What if the power of DeepMind were used to create biological weapons? In 2022, the Swiss government's Spiez Laboratory held a conference to study the use of AI to "design toxic molecules" and create an entirely new breed of chemical and biological weapons. This is when AI becomes truly scary, but someone has to ask these tough questions. The laboratory needed only six hours to generate forty thousand molecules deemed lethal to human beings, including VX nerve gas, as well as entirely new designs. All of this was created using AI tools broadly available by accessing public chemistry databases. In the end, the conference deemed it essential to limit public access to certain data that could be used by rogue states or individuals to easily invent the next generation of chemical and biological weapons, with no known antidotes or cures. They further identified the need for an international organization to monitor and police such activities, even as myriad corporations and countries embark on their own AI "tools" that feed off available data.

Should a specific country's AI be poorly designed, using publicly available data as well as garbage data, then AI "hallucinations" could become the norm, spreading broadly across international bad actors. AI-powered missiles, especially nuclear ones, are the greatest fear. One need only remember the Terminator movies and how Skynet wrought devastation and near human extinction when its AI computer reached sentience—and that was in 1984! Nearly forty years later, have we learned nothing?

It's time to step back and think about what we're doing for a brief moment. That is, while there is still time.

We've often thought of our brains as computers, though little is known about how our brains truly work. But nerve cells, signals, and neurotransmitters are far more complex than we imagine, as research into the eighty-six to a hundred billion neurons in the average brain has shown. The most abundant and important of these are glial cells, the brain's "secretarial pool." Glial cells insulate, protect, and support neuron functions, maintain homeostasis, and form myelin, regulating the flow of blood and "cleaning up" debris when someone suffers a major brain injury. Alzheimer's and Parkinson's disease as well as multiple sclerosis are all tied to glial cell dysfunction. In essence, our brain's neurons are the computer network, and the glial cells its operating system, virus protection, and network administrator.

After Albert Einstein died in 1955, his brain disappeared. Pathologist Thomas Harvey performed the postmortem autopsy on Einstein and weighed the brilliant physicist's brain at 1,230 grams—remarkably, smaller and lighter than the average brain! Then Dr. Harvey took Einstein's brain on a strange adventure, regularly cutting off samples for slides and eventually keeping the brain in a jar inside a cider box in his home. When it was "rediscovered" in 1994, the dissected brain was returned to Einstein's heirs, who donated it to Mutter Medical Museum in Philadelphia. After forty years, we finally know what made Einstein so smart: glial cells. Though Einstein's brain weighed less than the average human brain, it was also 15 percent wider and featured an additional ridge along its mid-frontal lobe, as well as more glial cells relative to neurons. Our mid-frontal lobe oversees planning and working memory, so researchers point to Einstein's "smaller" brain as being profoundly productive due to these anomalies, including extra glial cells to monitor and maintain high function.

Comparing Einstein's brain to today's AI may sound melodramatic, but it highlights the critical importance of structure and data. This is when the global innovation system is most critical. While AI promises warp-speed advances, it also raises real concerns that what it finds could be revealed too quickly to be contained (chemical, biological, and nuclear weapons included). True research and, yes, the boring work of experts debating standards, ethics, compliance, and other unforeseen issues are essential. Doing so will give us all greater security while widening the gap between those inside the global innovation ecosystem and those outside.

In June 2023, Alphabet (the parent company of both Google and DeepMind) announced the launch of Anti Money Laundering AI after a successful test with international banking giant HSBC. This AI program promises to clean up international banking with faster identification of suspicious funds while batch processing hundreds of thousands of transactions each day.

HSBC is also using AI and quantum computing for customer logins and corporate security. Now, consider the North Korean hacker who tries to gain access to HSBC's accounts in 2023 compared to the hacking of Bangladesh's national bank in 2016. The learning curve will be steep, especially as North Korea remains insulated from outsiders in the global innovation ecosystem. Would China share its AI breakthroughs with neighboring North Korean hackers who might turn those same tools against them?

In 2010, a simple programmable logic controller running Microsoft Windows was enough to totally disable Iran's nuclear ambitions. In place of the Stuxnet virus, imagine a cyberattack by an AI tool comparable to DeepMind. Innumerable cyber experts trying to stop such an attack would be no match for the reinforced learning of DeepMind, which can compute tens of millions of calculations per second. Now imagine a curious terrorist playing with a publicly accessible AI tool to create new molecules and suddenly stumbling on VX nerve gas or, worse, an easily deployed biological weapon with no known cure.

This echoes the moment when the first fire lance appeared on a battlefield: shiny, yet ancient armor against an inconceivable new weapon with no known defense. The moment when the proud Roman legions looked to the Alps only to see Hannibal's war elephants on the march. Battle as we know it will never be the same. Those who fail to adapt, share, or collaborate will fall behind. And those who fail to create standards, ethics, compliance, and governance will create a risk for everyone.

On October 30, 2023, the Biden Administration became the first major government to take steps toward the "safe, secure, and trustworthy development and use of artificial intelligence." Via executive order, the United States put the National Institute of Standards and Technology in charge of guiding the governmental and commercial development of this risky yet beneficial breakthrough innovation by creating an AI risk management framework for its development and deployment. By both encouraging and trying to control AI, the United States made clear that civil rights, privacy, education, and protections for workers will be paramount, while also allowing businesses and the military to unlock AI's potential for good by promoting a common approach to its many challenges. However new, this order will have broad implications domestically and internationally, while also leaving room for true innovation without strangulation via government overregulation.

This is only the beginning. Yes, AI will replace jobs. Ironically, software developers are considered the first to be vulnerable. But this hasn't held true. According to a 2017 study by Evans Data Corporation, 17.7 million software developers were employed worldwide, and around 28 million were needed by the end of 2023. Industry experts now admit that the projected 17 percent increase in demand was in fact 25 percent, with around 40 million software developers needed by 2030. AI certainly brings greater efficiency to coding, via automatic scripts and faster rendering, yet human brains are still required for the foreseeable future.

Customer service is another area deemed easily automated via AI, through chatbots and rerouting of customer needs and inquiries, for many major corporations. But customers—actual human beings—already complain that communicating with AI is neither pleasant nor efficient, forcing companies to rethink rapid AI automation of critical business functions. While redundant tasks classified as "cut and paste" functions will be replaced with automation—akin to assembly line operations and robots—there is no replacement for a fully engaged human brain focused on a meaningful job.

It seems that the faster we try to embrace AI, the more questions we raise. Elon Musk may question and try to limit AI, but his most popular company is an AI tool. Tesla isn't a car company at all; it launches nodes (cars) around the world that upload their data to Tesla to improve its self-driving capabilities. Self-driving cars will soon evolve; "smart" homes and office security will be monitored by artificial intelligence 24/7. Unmanned drones are already worldwide, with potentially deadly implications should AI run amok. Could our government representatives soon be replaced by AI, with direct surveys from voters selecting policy and elections? Do our leaders dare consider their positions as replaceable while weighing the overall impact of AI?

Is this the future we want? AI has been a subject for decades, and we've already witnessed multiple stages in its development that have been replete with promise and terror, breakthroughs and dead ends.

I remember wandering through the historic cobblestone streets of Prague in the summer of 2019. I soon found myself in an animated conversation with a young tech enthusiast named Lukas. His fervor about the future of artificial intelligence was palpable, juxtaposed against a backdrop of the city's centuries-old architecture—the ancient meets the ultramodern. His vision of a European renaissance through AI captured my imagination, and I felt the stirrings of an impending revolution. Yet, within a few years, the global AI landscape has shifted dramatically, echoing the ebbs and flows of political and economic tides. The fact remains that we truly cannot predict what's coming until it's too late.

Artificial intelligence promises unfathomable advances in medicine, productivity, and warfare. Now, before innumerable AI tools are launched by countries and companies, is the time to offer some guardrails, ethics, and compliance. While banking institutions may already see the potential of AI to prevent illegal money laundering via hackers, much more is at risk: security and actual human lives. Now is the moment, when others will look back and know whether we took action or allowed chaos to be unleashed.

BIBLIOGRAPHY

Al-Sibai, Noor. "Stanford Scientists Find That Yes, ChatGPT is Getting Stupider." *Futurism*, July 20, 2023. https://futurism.com/the-byte/stanford-chatgpt-getting-dumber.

Anolytics. "8 Data Types That Major AI Models Feed on to Function." February 14, 2023. https://www.anolytics.ai/blog/top-8-data-types-that-major-ai-models-feed-on-to-function/.

Bendett, Samuel. "Russia's Artificial Intelligence Boom May Not Survive the War." *Defense One*, April 15, 2022. https://www.defenseone.com/ideas/2022/04/russias-artificial-intelligence-boom-may-not-survive-war/365743/.

Bloom, David. "The WGA Reached a Tentative Deal. Here's What Happens Next." *Forbes*, September 25, 2023. https://www.forbes.com/sites/dbloom/2023/09/25/the-wga-reached-a-tentative-deal-heres-what-happens-next/?sh=29668d42375b.

Forbes. "How Real People Are Caught Up in Reddit's Porn." May 11, 2023. https://www.forbes.com/sites/rashishrivastava/2023/05/11/reddit-ai-generated-porn/?sh=58dd721b2e52 .

Kaminsky, Natalie, Ofer Bihari, Sivan Kanner, and Ari Barzilai. "Connecting Malfunctioning Glial Cells and Brain Degenerative Disorders." *Genomics Proteomics Bioinformatics* 14, no. 3 (June 2016). https://www.ncbi.nlm.nih.gov/pmc/articles/PMC4936608/.

Kolirin, Lianne. "Artist Rejects Photo Prize after AI-Generated Image Wins Award." *CNN*, April 18, 2023. https://www.cnn.com/style/article/ai-photo-win-sony-scli-intl/index.html.

Mangan, Dan. "Judge Sanctions Lawyers for Brief Written by A.I. with Fake Citations." *CNBC*, June 22 2023. https://www.cnbc.com/2023/06/22/judge-sanctions-lawyers-whose-ai-written-filing-contained-fake-citations.html.

Markel, Howard. "The Strange Story of Einstein's Brain." *PBS News Hour*, April 19, 2023. https://www.pbs.org/newshour/health/the-strange-story-of-einsteins-brain.

Neill, Bridget, John Hallmark, Richard Jackson, and Dan Diasio. "Key Takeaways from the Biden Administration Executive Order on AI." Ernst & Young, October 31, 2023. https://www.ey.com/en_us/public-policy/key-takeaways-from-the-biden-administration-executive-order-on-ai.

Sundar, Sindhu, and Aaron Mok. "What Is ChatGPT? Here's Everything You Need to Know about ChatGPT, the Chatbot Everyone's Still Talking About." *Business Insider*, August 21, 2023. https://www.businessinsider.com/everything-you-need-to-know-about-chat-gpt-2023-1.

Taylor, Josh, and Dan Milmo. "How Twitter's New Drastic Changes Will Affect What Users Can View on the Site." *The Guardian*, July 3, 2023. https://www.theguardian.com/technology/2023/jul/03/how-twitter-new-changes-will-affect-users-rate-limited-limit-exceeded-restrictions.

Tokar, Dylan. "Google Cloud Launches Anti-Money-Laundering Tool for Banks, Betting on the Power of AI." *Wall Street Journal*, June 21, 2023. https://www.wsj.com/articles/google-cloud-launches-anti-money-laundering-tool-for-banks-betting-on-the-power-of-ai-2512ccce.

Urbina, Fabio, Filippa Lentzos, Cédric Invernizzi, and Sean Ekins. "Dual Use of Artificial-Intelligence-Powered Drug Discovery." *Nature Machine Intelligence* 4 (2022). https://www.nature.com/articles/s42256-022-00465-9.

Villasenor, John. "Artificial Intelligence and the Future of Geopolitics." Brookings Institution, November 14, 2018. https://www.brookings.edu/articles/artificial-intelligence-and-the-future-of-geopolitics/.

Vita, Aelia. "How Many Software Developers Are There in the World?" Aster Cloud, November 18, 2021. https://aster.cloud/2021/11/18/how-many-software-developers-are-there-in-the-world/.

Wetsman, Nicole, "Alphabet Is Launching a Company That Uses AI for Drug Discovery," *The Verge*, November 4, 2021. https://www.theverge.com/2021/11/4/22763535/google-alphabet-drug-discovery-deepmind-ai.

Zauderer, Steven. "Artificial Intelligence Statistics & Facts for 2023." Cross River Therapy, July 23, 2023. https://www.crossrivertherapy.com/research/artificial-intelligence-statistics.

9

Qatar, the United Arab Emirates, and Saudi Arabia

Leading the World in Sustainability

In 1916, a secret meeting between French and British officials effectively erased what had long been accepted as the tribal and national borders of the Near East. The resulting Sykes–Picot Agreement carved up the region, ignoring religious, cultural, and social differences, as well as the self-determination rights of millions of ancient peoples. The collapse of the Ottoman Empire in 1918 only added to colonizers' greed and antipathy toward native Middle Easterners. Imperial interests were the focus, ignoring the realities of the region, including both existing allegiances and the differences among peoples, languages spoken, and religious beliefs.

In 1918, a map of the region was drawn by none other than T. E. Lawrence (aka Lawrence of Arabia). Keenly aware that religious differences were a primary cause of conflict in the Middle East (especially between Shia and Sunni Muslims), Lawrence knew these centuries-old clashes would only continue if not recognized with individual, separate countries. Lawrence recommended "Irak" be split in two, between Sunni Kurds and Shia Muslims. His map, and his insights into the people of the Middle East, were ignored by his British superiors.

In 2018, exactly one hundred years later, I found myself in the sizzling heat of a summer afternoon in Dubai, haggling over antique maps that captured a rich tapestry of the Middle East's history. The market vendor, a silver-bearded man named Ibrahim, pointed to a curious-looking map that dated to the early twentieth century. As he narrated the tale of the Sykes–Picot Agreement, it struck me how arbitrary lines had reshaped destinies, and how those decisions still echo today. Those old maps had been redrawn by colonizers to perpetuate domestic unrest, undermining these amazing people, determining their fates from afar.

The discovery of vast oil reserves, combined with easily stirred religious and domestic unrest, have allowed former colonizers, then superpowers and corporations, to take advantage of the mostly Muslim Middle East, its natural resources, and especially its people. With Israel in the mix, the region has rarely known peace. But after the United States' clumsy retreat from Afghanistan and Russia's invasion of Ukraine, Arab leaders now have an independent, semi-protectionist, and regionalistic attitude. The oil-rich nations of the Middle East are no longer so trusting of long-held allies, nor so easily manipulated by distant powers.

Instead, they are turning to one another and using innovation to settle ancient conflicts and create a more sustainable ecosystem. A new Middle East is emerging as a key broker for peace, with some of the most aggressive innovation initiatives underway in tandem, including clean energy, space travel, overlooked niche technologies, and impressive consumer gadgets. In only a handful of years, Qatar, the United Arab Emirates (UAE), and Saudi Arabia have created their own innovation ecosystems to reinvent both their economies and futures.

The wealthy Middle East is capable of attracting the brightest minds and best companies around the world, creating entirely new cities focused on innovation. The hyper-speed evolution of the region has been hastened by a new generation of leaders who have learned from the successes and failures of other countries highlighted in this book, and I am incredibly proud and humbled to have been part of this transformation. It's rare to meet with multiple ministers from nations who are so aware of their present status, needs, and dreams, so eager to embark on a mission to build anew. They know that tomorrow is coming fast, and there's no time to delay.

The term "Silicon Valley" was first coined in 1971, then developed over decades into the high-tech powerhouse of the West. The Middle East has laid the foundation for its own version of Silicon Valley in less than ten years. It's not a coincidence that these innovation initiatives are occurring where the world has fed its lust for crude oil for a century. These leaders know that amid unpredictable international oil prices, they must diversify for their own economic stability and growth. Add dwindling water supplies and increased international insecurity, and Qatar, the UAE, and Saudi Arabia have made innovation a priority to survive.

Qatar found glory as host of the 2022 FIFA World Cup, spending a remarkable $220 billion to host 1.4 million soccer fans and 1.5 billion global viewers. The smallest country to ever host this major international event, Qatar spent fifteen times more money than the previous host, Russia, and used the opportunity to take full advantage of the world's attention. The result was seven new cutting-edge stadiums, plus the full renovation of another, and ten new hotels. The World Cup was a spectacular success, and Argentina beat France on nail-biting penalty kicks.

Endeavors that culminate in massive new development don't happen overnight. Nor was Qatar solely focused on soccer; they parlayed the attention and investment into sustainable infrastructure for future high-tech innovation. In 2010, before Qatar was selected to host the World Cup, its Gulf Organization for Research and Development was hard at work, proving that the country could manage over one million tourists, thousands of broadcasters, and hundreds of professional athletes, especially in Qatar's stifling heat. That proof resulted in entirely new environmental and architectural ideas (one stadium was built of 974 shipping containers, which happens to be Qatar's area code), with a focus on recycling and "clean tech," touting 45 percent less water and energy consumption than older designs. A skeptical writer for *The Guardian* later admitted that "the first such showpiece staged in the Middle East not only looks miles ahead of the curve, but a decent template for major twenty-first-century high-density sporting events."

The buildings were only the beginning.

Qatar's Mobility Innovations Center created a unique series of sensors that allowed millions of visitors to access the internet for real-time updates and scores, and vital information including traffic updates and the best routes from the capital of Doha to the assorted stadiums scattered around the country. Qatar may only be the size of Cyprus, but bringing high-speed data connections across 11,570 square kilometers to millions of people who speak twenty different languages was no small feat. Qatar's Hamad Bin Khalifa University is now adapting these sensors as an inexpensive way to virtually monitor the vital signs of athletes, hospital patients, and the elderly, which has vast potential for commercial exporting and revenues.

Adapting existing technologies into something new and extraordinary is the definition of innovation. The Qatar Science & Technology Park is both a hub and an incubator for such ideas. One company to emerge is Bonocle, which has developed an entertainment system for the blind, sight-impaired, and disabled. Bonocle incorporates a "Braille cell" into a small device that can be operated with one hand, empowering anyone to read, write, count, measure and, of course, play games.

Innovation is now so enmeshed into Qatari culture that it has become popular entertainment—*Stars of Science* is the country's longest-running reality TV show. Thousands of inventors apply to take part in the show's twelve-week competition; winning ideas include a free Wi-Fi platform and a home-cooking robot named Oliver. More than just entertainment, Qatar has made innovation cross-cultural and cool; inventors and entrepreneurs are celebrities to be lauded and encouraged. The result is an otherwise small country that fosters and grows its own innovation ecosystem, becoming a marvel that the world watches, embraces, and invests in.

When China was forced to forfeit its right to host the 2023 Asian Football Cup (due to its zero-COVID policies), Qatar was more than happy to step in, given its well-planned sporting and hospitality capacity after the 2022 World Cup. Sustainability has been at the forefront of Qatar's efforts, which dictate that everything built must be reusable. Additional construction materials and recycled shipping containers, even extra stadium seats and soccer equipment, have all been donated to needy nations. Education City Stadium will remain standing, a beacon for Qatar's nine different universities and eleven schools, just one of a number of byproducts of Qatar using the World Cup to build infrastructure for a cutting-edge national future.

Inspired by its infrastructure and higher international visibility, Qatar is setting its sights on the stars. The Qatar Aeronautics and Space Agency (QASA) has partnered with NASA to launch a specialized scientific satellite, promising sustainable and peaceful efforts in outer space for all nations. While some point to ties with Iran as concern for an arms race in space, Qatar's National Vision 2030 has made clear that its innovations in missile, satellite, and scientific technologies will be solely intended to develop experts in the field for peaceful learning and exploration.

Politically, Qatar is a semi-constitutional monarchy, with close ties to Iran due to their shared ownership of the South Pars/North Dome gas field—the largest natural gas field in the world, with over fifty trillion cubic meters of reserves. Qatar's population is 90 percent Sunni Muslim, and its relations with Iran are both economic and religious, dating back to the Iran–Iraq War. Saudi Arabia, another neighbor with a Sunni majority population, has had a decades-long ongoing and mostly nonmilitary conflict over regional influence with Qatar, known as the New Arab Cold War. Qatar and the UAE, another Sunni majority neighbor, had a brief diplomatic spat in 2017 but restored ties in 2021.

Qatar is the wealthiest country per capita in the Middle East, with an average income of $183,100 per Qatari citizen. Its semi-constitutional government allows for rapid dictates, massive government financing, and prompt enforcement. Qatar has proven—as shown before and during the 2022 World Cup—that it can accomplish anything deemed essential to its economy and security. Foreign investors and high-tech companies find an especially warm welcome in Qatar; those who try to sway this small country's proudly independent leaders will find more of a challenge.

This came to the fore in 2020 when Saudi Arabia and the UAE tried to blockade Qatar as punishment for its support of Iran and other nonstate rogue actors in the region. Strangely, the situation also involved an office building in Manhattan owned by Jared Kushner (son-in-law of then-president Donald

Trump). The blockade was launched, with America's approval, only weeks after the Kushners failed to sell their office building to Qatar's minister of finance. Then the blockade conveniently ended after Qatar brokered a favorable deal to bail out the Kushner property. These are the stakes in the region—odd players and big money included—which explain why many Middle Eastern countries remain wary of outside influences.

To Qatar's south lies the United Arab Emirates, one of the most unique countries in the Middle East and a leader in tourism and clean-tech innovation. Governed as a "tribal autocracy" by seven constituent monarchies, the UAE boasts the sixth-largest oil reserves in the world. It has a population of just under ten million and a GDP of a half-trillion dollars, making it among the wealthiest and largest economies in the region. Bridging the Persian Gulf and Gulf of Oman, the UAE has historically been known as an open economy, welcoming tourism, trade, and investment.

Development has been a key focus domestically, with no less than $350 billion in construction projects underway in the UAE at any given moment. Dubai is a marvel, with shimmering skyscrapers, megamalls, and desert excursions, claiming the prize as the fourth most popular city in the world for tourists (just behind Germany and the United Kingdom for total annual visitors). Massive construction and millions of tourists come at an environmental cost, however, so the UAE is underwriting multiple innovation hubs focused on clean technology.

In 2018, the UAE National Strategy for Advanced Innovation clearly laid out technical hubs and clusters across the country with a focus on smarter, sustainable urban living and development. The materials, energy, and water usage are highly efficient; even the buildings and furniture at Tech Park are made from recycled plastics and shipping containers. Scalability of new innovations is a key focus, as the UAE wants to be both a regional and global leader in clean tech. The Annual Climate Innovations Exchange (CLIX) summit, sponsored and hosted by the UAE, draws attention and attendees from around the world. The last CLIX summit received 811 applications from 83 different countries, bringing inventors and private investors together with sustainability as a shared goal.

Renewable and clean energy are now ways of life in the UAE. When the Mohammed bin Rashid Al Maktoum Solar Park is completed in 2030, it will be the largest independent power producer in the world (at 5,000 megawatts), saving 6.5 million tons of carbon emissions annually. Nuclear power is another focus; five new plants are being built across the country to help offset the high energy demands of connected water desalination plants. This oil-rich country is investing even more money to create a multibillion-dollar fund to spur clean-energy developments around the world, estimated to have drawn promises of up to $25 billion total.

Beyond new infrastructure and investment, what the UAE and most Middle Eastern nations see as the major hindrance to innovation is a lack of technical developers. Coders and integrators are in high demand, yet are sorely lacking in the region. New training programs and immigration policies must be created and reformed to successfully grow a sustainable innovation ecosystem across the UAE and Middle East. Israel's mass migration of Jews helped that country to grow and prosper, especially its technical talent, but that is a singular example that other Middle Eastern countries cannot copy. Attracting talent remains a challenge, so domestic technical training programs must grow as migration incentives are put into place.

Saudi Arabia is the cornerstone for solving these regional issues and may be the catalyst for much more. The kingdom has the greatest influence over the Middle East and now enjoys the world's stage. Crown Prince Mohammed bin Salman has emerged as the de facto leader of the world's biggest oil exporter, and his influence is rapidly spreading far beyond the region. The House of Saud has ruled the territory known as Saudi Arabia since 1720, and the family's net worth is estimated at around $1.4 trillion. To put this in perspective, combining the total wealth of the top ten richest people on Earth would still not equal the known holdings of the House of Saud.

Saudi Arabia has been tied to the economic policies and military strategies of the West for the past century. Other than Israel, no other Middle Eastern country has better relations with the United Kingdom and the United States. But times have changed, with massive implications for both sides.

The United States' domestic production of oil has weakened its otherwise strong economic ties, with Saudi crude oil exports to the United States falling to $16.6 billion in 2022, compared to over $50 billion ten years earlier. As the United States has become a net oil exporter, its influence over oil exporters in the Middle East has softened. Meanwhile, China has bought the oil that the United States used to import, accounting for $65 billion in Saudi Arabia crude exports in 2022. Currently, Russia and Saudi Arabia are the primary suppliers of oil to China, but Russia's oil is sold at a steep discount, due to its invasion of Ukraine and international sanctions. OPEC (Organization of Petroleum Exporting Countries) member nations are struggling to reach consensus on whether to cut or increase supplies, while Saudi Arabia has shown an independence that is both troubling for long-held allies and inspiring for emerging economies.

In March 2023 Iran, Saudi Arabia's nemesis, suddenly restored relations in negotiations brokered by China, sending shock waves around the world. Moreover, Israel has been invited to be part of Saudi Arabia's futuristic NEOM urban innovation city, bringing the finest minds in technology to the Tabuk Province to collaborate. The Russia–Ukraine War (nearing two years of devastation at the time of writing) may soon reach a truce, with peace talks hosted by Saudi Arabia and again brokered by China. All global events suddenly seem to be centered around Saudi Arabia, with the young crown prince seizing his moment to invent a new future.

Invent is the operative word.

The crown prince represents a new generation of leaders aware of the need to diversify economies for greater security. Crude oil prices have been on a wild ride, falling into the negative during the COVID-19 pandemic (in April 2020, West Texas crude was priced at -$37.63 per barrel and OPEC, $12.22 per barrel), to over $120 per barrel during Russia's invasion of Ukraine in February 2022. The business of big oil has been unpredictable, so Saudi Arabia is wise to balance its economy via innovation, job-training programs, and exports other than oil.

This isn't the ancient House of Saud; it's a rapidly evolving country with the motivation and funding to quickly dictate and develop. Saudi Arabia is investing $40 billion to achieve 70 percent of its energy capacity as renewable by 2030 and to be fully carbon neutral by 2050. The King Abdullah University of Science and Technology and the Prince Mohammed bin Salman bin Abdulaziz University for Digital Science and Technology are just two innovation hubs that are part of the much larger National Transformation Program and Vision 2030. Jobs, science, and technology are the focus, with a goal of $16 billion in new R&D spending by 2040.

These are lofty plans, and Saudi Arabia has a long way to go. Saudi Arabia ranked sixty-sixth out of 132 economies on the Global Innovation Index; Qatar ranked fifty-two, the UAE ranked thirty-one, and Israel ranked sixteen. Saudi leaders sense the urgency to keep up with the pack, and have attracted $40 billion in investment to create twenty thousand jobs to work in an "innovation ecosystem." Sound familiar?

In June 2023 the NEOM urban tech hub, presently under construction, announced $21 billion in new funding. Partners are lining up, including a new data center for Microsoft and a cloud computing venture with Google. Israel is also involved, highlighting the breadth and openness of the venture as the Middle East and high-tech leaders look to NEOM as a fresh opportunity to collaborate and innovate. "Human progress" is one goal of NEOM, and sustainable building in the age of climate change will be another, in addition to AI. While some skeptics point to Saudi Arabia's lax data security laws as cause for concern, partners in NEOM are intent on using the venture to address and rewrite the rules—this is a rare opportunity to begin anew. Attracting talent will be critical, as tech developers from abroad must abide by and adapt to the country's social and political structure in order to work in the world's most advanced ecosystem. Money is no problem for the kingdom, which offers contracts and salaries far beyond those found in Silicon Valley. Still, there is an enormous difference between northern California and northern Saudi Arabia, so NEOM's future hinges on offering the diversity and openness essential to fostering innovation.

A new Middle East is emerging, focused on the realities facing everyone involved: water shortages, sustainable building, exploding tourism, and the vast potential of solar power, AI, and data, combined with the need to collaborate peacefully while diversifying from solely oil-based economies. New construction is underway, wisely based on recycling and efficiency; even former enemies are now considered partners in these rapid advances. In late August 2023, the BRICS bloc (originally Brazil, Russia, India, China, and South Africa) admitted Saudi Arabia, the UAE, Iran, Egypt, and Argentina as members, with the stated goal of reshuffling the global power structures to champion the "Global South."

We are witnessing multiple innovation ecosystems being built in real time, interconnected by shared needs, with true regional and international partnerships being forged. In addition to hosting major international sporting events, perhaps the Middle East is showing Africa, Southeast Asia, and South America a new path forward, focused on collaboration and innovation? In the next ten years, we will see more global advancements coming from the Middle East than from any other region, as these innovation ecosystems enmesh, then propagate ideas.

I am often in the Middle East. I like to walk through the gleaming corridors of Qatar's stadiums, so new and proud after the FIFA World Cup, sensing and seeing the stark juxtaposition between the ancient and the modern. How they manage to coexist tells the tale of a region that is reclaiming its narrative. From the skyscrapers of the UAE to the innovation hubs of Saudi Arabia, I have witnessed in real time a transformation that is both breathtaking and profound.

Somewhere Lawrence of Arabia is smiling, as the Middle East that he envisioned a century ago now emerges, inspired and empowered, collaborating to solve shared problems and invent a sustainable future.

BIBLIOGRAPHY

2020 GE Global Innovation Barometer. "Saudi Arabia Executive Report," January and September 2020. https://www.ge.com/sites/default/files/GE_Global_Innovation_Barometer_2020-Saudi_Arabia_Country_Report.pdf.

Abdallah, Samer. "How to Pioneer Innovation and Economic Transformation in Saudi Arabia." *Wamda*, June 1, 2023. https://www.wamda.com/2023/06/pioneer-innovation-economic-transformation-saudi-arabia.

Awad, Salam. "A Glimpse of Life in the Middle East before Colonial Borders." *Middle East Eye*, March 11, 2022. https://www.middleeasteye.net/discover/middle-east-life-glimpse-before-colonial-borders-pictures.

Baker, Aryn. "Here's What Will Happen to Qatar's Billion Dollar Stadiums Now That the World Cup Is Over." *Time*, December 20, 2022. https://time.com/6242292/what-happens-to-qatar-world-cup-stadiums/.
BBC News. "Saudi Crown Prince Mohammed bin Salman, Power behind the Throne." October 6, 2020. https://www.bbc.com/news/world-middle-east-40354415.
BBC News. "World Cup 2022: How Has Qatar Treated Foreign Workers?" November 9, 2022. https://www.bbc.com/news/world-60867042.
Bloomberg News. "What Qatar Built for the World's Most Expensive World Cup Ever." November 18, 2022. https://www.bloomberg.com/graphics/2022-what-qatar-built-for-the-world-cup/#xj4y7vzkg.
Coleman, Zach, and Karl Mathiesen. "Wealthy Oil Nation Lays Groundwork for 'Eye-Popping' Climate Fund." *Politico*, August 18, 2023. https://www.politico.com/news/2023/08/18/united-arab-emirates-eye-popping-climate-fund-00111736.
du Plessis, Carien, Anait Miridzhanian, and Acharya Bhargav. "BRICS Welcomes New Members in Push to Reshuffle World Order." *Reuters*, August 24, 2023. https://www.reuters.com/world/brics-poised-invite-new-members-join-bloc-sources-2023-08-24/.
EuroNews. "Fostering Innovation, the Qatar Way." May 10, 2022. https://www.euronews.com/2022/10/05/fostering-innovation-the-qatar-way.
Goodman, Ryan, and Julia Brooks. "Timeline on Jared Kushner, Qatar, 666 Fifth Avenue, and White House Policy." *Just Security*, March 11, 2020. https://www.justsecurity.org/69094/timeline-on-jared-kushner-qatar-666-fifth-avenue-and-white-house-policy/.
Hack, Kevin, and Jimmy Troderman. "Crude Oil Prices Rise Above $100 Per Barrel after Russia's Further Invasion into Ukraine." US Energy Information Administration, March 4, 2022. https://www.eia.gov/todayinenergy/detail.php?id=51498.
Hijjawi, Anas. "Innovation Nation: How the UAE Is Establishing Itself as a Global Frontrunner in Game-Changing Technologies." *Entrepreneur*, December 2, 2022. https://www.entrepreneur.com/en-ae/technology/innovation-nation-how-the-uae-is-establishing-itself-as-a/439954.
Ibrahim, Menatalla. "Qatar Urges World Powers to Ensure 'Sustainable, Peaceful' Use of Outer Space." *Doha News*, February 9, 2023. https://dohanews.co/qatar-urges-world-powers-to-ensure-sustainable-peaceful-use-of-outer-space/.
Katulis, Brian, Ross Harrison, Gerald M. Feierstein, et al. "10 Key Events and Trends in the Middle East and North Africa in 2022." *Middle East Institute*, December 19, 2022. https://mei.edu/publications/10-key-events-and-trends-middle-east-and-north-africa-2022#harrison.
Moss, Sebastian. "Despite Climate Pledge, Google Partners with World's Largest Oil Company for Saudi Cloud Region." *Data Center Dynamics*, December 22, 2020. https://www.datacenterdynamics.com/en/news/despite-climate-pledge-google-partners-worlds-largest-oil-company-saudi-cloud-region/.
Murphy, Cullen, and Haisam Hussein. "Lines in the Sand." *Vanity Fair*, January 2008. https://www.vanityfair.com/news/2008/01/middle-east-cultural-political-map.
O'Neill, Aaron. "MENA Region: Gross Domestic Product (GDP) in 2022, by Country." Statista.com, August 29, 2023. https://www.statista.com/statistics/804761/gdp-of-the-mena-countries/.

Qatar Foundation for Scientific American Custom Media. "How the World Cup Is Driving Qatari Innovation." *Scientific American*. Accessed August 2, 2023. https://www.scientificamerican.com/custom-media/a-new-dawn-for-innovation-in-qatar/how-the-world-cup-is-driving-qatari-innovation/.

Reuters."Qatar, Iran Share World's Biggest Gas Field." July 26, 2010. https://www.reuters.com/article/us-northfield-qatar/factbox-qatar-iran-share-worlds-biggest-gas-field-idUSTRE66P1VV20100726.

US Energy Information Administration. "Oil and Petroleum Products Explained." October 2, 2023. https://www.eia.gov/energyexplained/oil-and-petroleum-products/imports-and-exports.php.

Vohra, Anchal. "The Pitiful Endgame of Saudi Arabia's Qatar Blockade." *Foreign Policy*, December 11, 2020. https://foreignpolicy.com/2020/12/11/the-pitiful-endgame-of-saudi-arabias-qatar-blockade/.

World Future Energy Summit. "UAE Plans to Become a Global Innovation Hub." Accessed September 5, 2023. https://www.worldfutureenergysummit.com/en-gb/future-insights-blog/uae-plans-to-become-a-global-innovation-hub.html.

World Intellectual Property Organization. "Global Innovation Index 2022: Switzerland, the US, and Sweden lead the Global Innovation Ranking; China Approaches Top 10; India and Türkiye Ramping Up Fast; Impact-Driven Innovation Needed in Turbulent Times." September 29, 2022. https://www.wipo.int/pressroom/en/articles/2022/article_0011.html.

10

Singapore

The Most Precious Passport

When's the last time you traveled internationally? My passport is full of stamps, as you would expect. What I'm lacking, however, is the ultimate prize.

My birthplace of Italy is ranked second on this list, tied with Germany and Spain, while my adopted home country of Britain is ranked fourth. The United States has been slipping for ten years straight, finding itself at eighth. Meanwhile, the lowest is also the least enviable, Afghanistan. Am I talking about innovation, new cutting-edge technology, or maybe the latest and greatest weapon? No. I'm talking about passports.

The global citizenship and residence advisory firm Henley & Partners compiles an annual index of "golden" passports. Passports and their respective benefits provide data on movement, business, international relations, and personal curiosity. Singapore's passport is the envy of those in the know. Anyone possessing a Singaporean passport enjoys visa-free access to 193 countries, putting the world in their grasp. The United States and the United Kingdom used to be tied for number one on this vaunted list, but fewer countries are willing to offer open access to these countries, for many of the reasons already cited in this book. China and Ukraine are on the rise, while Russia's welcome abroad is in freefall.

In 1994, only 10 percent of Americans had a passport. Today, over 40 percent of Americans do, mostly because Canada, Mexico, and even some states require official government passports, either to enter or as identification. Still, that leaves 60 percent of Americans with no intention, nor ability, to travel internationally. Compare this to Europe, where border-crossing is the norm (including eased passport restrictions in the Eurozone). It's little wonder that Americans are sometimes viewed as overtly insular with little interest in, or exposure to, the world outside their country. Thankfully, this doesn't include the innumerable American technicians, researchers, and scientists, as well as corporate, university, and government officials, who share their work, findings, innovations, and investments globally.

So, what is Singapore doing so very well that 193 other countries openly welcome their citizens? The answer is easy: regulatory sandboxes.

In addition to the thorough case studies of specific countries in this book, I conclude with perhaps the most valuable lesson from one more, in addition to a solution to the many problems posited within. Our overriding concerns with innovation, AI, military, and the latest as-yet-unknown invention should be how they impact others. Brilliantly, Singapore has evolved its government's interaction with business to a point that the nation is both successful and trusted. Safety for the common good must be paramount, so Singapore found a solution.

Any new company that tries to enter Singapore's fintech (financial tech) economy is put in a regulatory sandbox for a brief period of time, usually a year or two. During that time, that company is in a "proof of concept" phase that encourages development while also intentionally containing its overall impact. Consider how impossible this would be in today's world, with myriad corporations racing to develop their own AI, never forgetting how many firms are eagerly developing munitions and weapons for the Ukraine–Russia conflict. This would never work—companies would quit altogether or, most likely, simply move to another country, one without such stringent controls.

But it works in Singapore, and with astonishing success. Fintech is the digitization of financial services and transactions: currencies, crypto, Bitcoin, and others included. Singapore has become the world leader in fintech without destroying its own economy. Considering the multiple implosions of "crypto" exchanges like FTX, it's amazing that any country focused on fostering alternative financial instruments and services isn't negatively impacted.

How?

Fintech and other startup firms eager to be part of Singapore's ascendance have been through the sandbox methodology: they benefit from relaxed government regulation, with less paperwork and bureaucracy, even as their technology is developed (provided, in a bit of a bubble). Once proven safe and effective, and in compliance with standards, these firms are released into the greater ecosystem, gaining funding while normal government controls become more stringent. This ensures these emerging companies and their products are viable and ethical players in the bigger marketplace.

While I have been to Singapore, I still await my golden passport. But what I have seen there is truly remarkable: highly motivated and brilliant fintech and technology developers taking so much risk, much like anywhere else, but with so much more at stake. For, should they prove their concept and get the approval of the government, they become "golden." Investors will flock to their company with funding because there is full confidence in their products and management. Equally critical is that any potentially disastrous side effects of a young inventor playing with cutting-edge technology have been minimized via the sandbox, offering an official seal of approval for the product's ultimate impact.

Try to imagine this in Silicon Valley. Or Beijing. Or London. Maybe in Israel, due to dual-use demands of companies by the government in the event of invasion. Very few countries would dare to be perceived as stifling any innovation, however briefly. Singapore has created an innovation ecosystem that provides a blueprint to solve many of the problems we are presently facing.

The result has exceeded expectations: Singapore is one of the most business-friendly and competitive markets in the world. Enjoying over 7 percent GDP growth and per capita incomes well above those of most developed countries, this is a highly connected nation in a critical part of the world. Exports rule, as does shipping and trade. Singapore's government pays foreign companies to train its population in IT, electronics, and petrochemicals. Consider the "invaluable" nature of Taiwan; Singapore is not far from a similar status, especially in the region.

This is when our story comes full circle. The notion of a sandbox is all too apt when seeking solutions to the world's many issues. International sanctions are a form of sandbox, to rein in rogue and aggressive states like Russia, Iran, and North Korea. To ensure compliance, we cut funding and illicit trade, as well as curtail unfriendly and toxic behavior. This is when the misbehaving child stands in the corner for a few minutes of "time out." I am not being coy when I suggest similar punishments are required for the few countries that make the world a worse place.

Now consider the same strategy for rogue nonstate actors, such as mercenaries and evil corporations. How to stop the spread of their malignancy? A sandbox isn't so simple when corporations can cross borders, especially as nation-states as we know them are erased due to the digital sphere. These rogue nonstate actors often survive in shadow economies, using illegal funds and clandestine communications. The easy solution is rejection; good-faith nations and organizations can refuse to work with or offer support to those aligned with bad actors. However, ignoring them is not an option; groups like al-Qaeda and Hamas are akin to toxic mold, growing and spreading in the darkness until discovered too late.

At its dawn is the time we may truly engage and influence the development of a nation, nonstate actor, corporation, organization, or even individual. It wouldn't be absurd to consider a United Nations of AI, which implies a global organization assigned to govern the development, standards, ethics, and compliance for artificial intelligence. Considering the Spiez Laboratory's shocking study of how easy it is for anyone with publicly available AI tools and data to potentially create biological and chemical weapons, I dare say we have no choice.

The military needs a sandbox too. The development of armaments is often so secretive that we only learn of their existence when horrified by their destructive capabilities on the battlefield. While neurotechnology may implant chips into the human brain, showing how a patient with Parkinson's disease can suddenly regain physical and mental capabilities, how will we feel when military soldiers sport similar implants, or wear war-ready exoskeletons? AI-powered computers can comb our unique molecular structures seeking designer cures for diseases or, maybe, accidentally creating new diseases. We have the technology and talent at our disposal to do good or ill, which means we also have an obligation to guide others with extreme vigilance. We need guardrails, standards, and governance.

A healthy global innovation ecosystem is the critical pillar and solution for improving living standards, societal structures, governance, connectivity, communication and, yes, security. We are on the verge of creating a massive gap between the haves and have-nots. Bluntly, some of those have-nots may be better off without advanced technology, especially considering the promised impact of quantum computing and true AI, never mind advanced weaponry. But this gap mustn't become an impossible chasm for others. In crucial regions like Nigeria, South Africa, most of the Middle East, and Southeast Asia, real people have all the ingredients to become world-leading innovators. All they lack is a spark: immigration reform that welcomes back talented and skilled former citizens to help rebuild their countries; better government with less corruption and more investment into R&D; greater collaboration with industry leaders.

Sometimes it only takes one element—one spark or enlightened government interaction with business—to inspire a revolution.

BIBLIOGRAPHY

Symons, Angela. "World's Most Powerful Passport: Germany, Italy and Spain Move Up into Second Place." *EuroNews*, July 20, 2023. https://www.euronews.com/travel/2023/07/20/worlds-most-powerful-passport-germany-italy-and-spain-move-up-into-second-place#

World Bank Group. The World Bank in Singapore. Accessed September 5, 2023. https://www.worldbank.org/en/country/singapore/

Zhou, Ping. "The History of Singapore's Economic Development." ThoughtCo.com, July 10, 2019. https://www.thoughtco.com/singapores-economic-development.

11

The Human Factor
Digital Alchemy

In the twilight of my twenties, I found myself standing in an underground vault beneath a centuries-old monastery in northern Italy, surrounded by scrolls and texts older than some civilizations. The guardian monk, a man of surprising technological awareness considering his austere surroundings, whispered, "Words are magic, and technology is our modern alchemy."

That chance encounter is what first led me down this rabbit hole of human evolution and our desire for transcendence through knowledge and innovation. As a security and technology specialist with boardroom and battlefield experience, I've learned that our tools and mediums may have evolved, but the human thirst for sharing and understanding remains constant.

As does inspiration.

Somewhere a scientist is playing with a lightsaber, possibly inspired by *Star Wars* and Luke Skywalker's famous fight with his father, Darth Vader. This film, released in 1977, sparked the imaginations of a generation of kids who later became scientists. Making lightsabers that can cut through metal and change colors like in the movies is now possible, using plasma instead of lasers.

Sci-fi books and movies have continually stirred our minds to invent. H. G. Wells was considered the first time traveler, with his many novels captivating turn-of-the-century readers over 125 years ago with stories about invisible men, alien invasions, the first men on the moon and, of course, time travel. We have already put men on the moon, and "invisible" suits are now a reality: interconnected wafers can copy the background landscape (a simple room or complex forest in full autumn bloom) and then display it in the foreground, virtually erasing the person wearing this magical cloak.

Remember when Ellen Ripley climbed into a robot exoskeleton to do battle with the Xenomorph? Released in 1979, the movie *Alien* warned us that no one can hear you scream in space, both terrifying and inspiring to a new generation of moviegoers and scientists. Today, those same exoskeletons are in use at air bases, military mostly, easily moving heavy cargo containers. This mechanized suit operated by one soldier can lift tons of weight and will soon be seen on battlefields. Being born in Italy, where Hannibal emerged from the Alps with war elephants, I can only imagine how troops will feel upon seeing an armored robot entering the fray.

We share so others know, to both warn and inspire. And there has never been a more crucial time to know, express, and collaborate than now. Nor has there ever been an easier time in human history to spread knowledge. With one click, screens big and small are updated around the world, whether with a cute picture or a GPS location from a drone sent on a secret mission. We are no longer smudging charcoal and ochre on cave walls in the hopes that others will find safe shelter and see them, but broadcasting serious news and scientific discoveries mixed with faint cries for attention to millions, even billions. It's all a bit overwhelming. The fear today is not whether we can share and collaborate for the common good, but whether anyone is even listening.

So, after digesting this book's contents, including innovation efforts, failures, and successes from over a dozen countries, where do you stand? Are you fully satisfied, resting on your laurels, gloating within the global innovation ecosystem as unknown rivals work tirelessly to eclipse your supposed excellence? Could you compete with that boy in Pakistan who has no choice but to complete his hand-cranked invention to bring clean water to his village?

What is your mission? Consider Olabanke Banjo, CEO of Cyrus45 Factory in Nigeria, who looked at millions of old discarded tires in her country and saw potential. Now those tires are being recycled into home flooring, insulated wall coverings, and furniture. They are rather beautiful, really: the world's waste in an underdeveloped country (albeit with oil revenues almost as massive as Nigeria's wealth disparities) is now the source material for a major employer and sustainable enterprise. This is just one of the many "sparks" of innovation that give us all hope, from an exceptional female leader who can inspire others in addition to providing jobs.

What is your urgency? I often think of how history repeats itself. How three hundred Spartans halted over a million Persian invaders; then, some 2,500 years later, thirty Ukrainians stopped a forty-mile Russia military envoy headed to Kyiv. If put in such a position, with overwhelming odds against you, could you be creative enough to survive?

Critically, ask yourself this: What is my present status? Am I sustaining, with ample budget and resources, talent and focus, to continue to succeed? If not, keep reading. If so, please remember that hubris is oftentimes the greatest of flaws.

Are you disruptive or breakthrough? Do you have enough intelligence about your competitors, enemies, and even neighbors, to know what their strengths and weaknesses are? If so, how can you offset or take advantage of both? As a case study, consider Israel (chapter 1); no other nation has existed under more dire circumstances, possessing the least, yet still survived and then thrived.

Still struggling, dependent on basic research and frugality? This is where many of us often feel in our daily lives. Plodding along, at times reliant on others' generosity, "borrowing" things but incapable of creating on our own. Fear not, hard work breeds personal ethos and wisdom. Know your worth while trying to ignore the impossible chasm that is slowly widening before you: when dependent on others, you have no choice in what they offer you. They may be withholding the one thing that will allow you to be fully liberated. "Teach a man to fish" is a lesson we all must learn, and this holds true in the age of hyperconnectivity and AI, as access to that one giant leap will make the difference between being a have or a have-not.

I am no Nostradamus. Yet my work sets me on the bleeding edge of new technology that is launched daily to influence and advance humankind—locally, nationally, regionally, globally, and of course, militarily. This is the future, and it is magic. With all of the bleak news being spread to draw attention (thus revenue), influence, or power for a country or leader, we rarely grasp all the good that is being conjured daily.

This is digital alchemy, and what I see is both exhilarating and terrifying.

It has only taken a few years for the public to become comfortable with unmanned drones, as either luxury toys or aerial surveillance for fun and policing. On the battlefield, however, a drone means both intelligence and action. The current generation of drones are highly maneuverable and lethal, with the technology still being proven—design and software glitches, as well as human error, still causing civilian casualties and death. Yet few fully grasp what drones will soon be capable of. In a recent competition held by the University of Zurich, the Swift AI (powered by artificial intelligence) drone won fifteen out of twenty-five races against the three top human drone-racing world champions. While it mostly avoided crashing on the three-dimensional course, the Swift AI drone clocked the fastest lap and handled accelerations up to five G-force (the speed at which a human being will black out). Remember this the next time videos of UFOs (now renamed UAPS—"unidentified anomalous phenomena") show unidentified craft moving at speeds far beyond those of modern military jets.

Now combine a drone with poorly developed AI with a bad actor like North Korea at the controls, and what we have is chaos. How do we manage this? Military contractors will continue to invent in the finest killing machines because that's what they are handsomely paid to do. While these toys and tools may be fun and incredibly effective, what happens if they are turned against us?

What's more troubling is where many eager nations are now turning: space.

Want to take down GPS worldwide? Or eliminate spy satellites, as well as those that only monitor weather or offer telecommunications? The answer is easy: make a mess in space. There are presently over twenty-seven thousand distinct pieces of orbital debris, or "space junk," zipping around the Earth. And each needs to be monitored because a single errant bolt or hunk of metal moving at 15,700 miles per hour will devastate a satellite or, worse, an international space station. Any serious collision could create thousands more chunks of junk that will forever orbit the Earth, forcing all other satellites to be rerouted. There may be no greater threat to future space travel, communications, and weather monitoring than a celestial junkyard that is impossible to escape.

Consider the recent report that China is testing a "space laser" with the purported capability of destroying satellites from Earth, or from other Chinese satellites in orbit, perhaps even attacking the Earth from space. Speculation rages, as does international condemnation. But the US Space Command was founded in 1985 for military operations in outer space, and the US Space Force was founded in 2019. The final frontier is obviously getting plenty of attention. And funding: Space Force's budget of $26.3 billion in 2023 exceeds the entire budget for NASA.

Whether in space, the sky, underwater, or on the ground, we must understand and, sadly, accept the impact of wars worldwide. Innocent civilians are caught in the middle; regional powers try to gain land and resources while also dealing with refugees fleeing the devastation; global powers in a proxy battle test new strategies and weapons. Our tax dollars are paying for wars big and small, so we all must take responsibility and exercise greater vigilance, whether sending aid or during elections.

I leave you with something perhaps more worrisome than space junk and AI run amok. This overdue and in-depth study of global innovation, players, and posers also raises a serious question about the future of countries versus companies. Data centers owned by countries and corporations are purposely being built in distant, often secretive, locations to avoid the laws of other countries. Our text messages, emails, and other data are being uploaded to satellites, then bounced over borders and across oceans within microseconds to curtail surveillance and tax levies. Our personal data is a gold mine for AI tools forever vacuuming up new information, while our brains struggle to make sense of so much information coming at us at once.

Countries and corporations eager to gain influence over each other regularly push for new technology, in the form of propaganda disguised as social media posts, to either distract or attract the interest of others. Disturbing as this may be, the goal is often to gain a highly emotional attachment to their targets. Most governments and organizations do this regularly. In August 2023, Facebook (certainly no innocent party in the spread of disinformation) announced the disruption of a vast "covert online influence operation" run by China, one with innumerable fake accounts spanning fifty different websites, including Facebook, YouTube, Twitter (now X), TikTok, and others. This was a well-designed and sprawling campaign of articles praising China, maligning US and EU policies, and attacking anyone who dared question China (or these policies). Mind you, this isn't the only campaign by a country or corporation, nor will it be the last.

Today, we are all targets in the new age of information warfare. Own and restrict your data like your life depends on it—because it does.

Wars begin and end through diplomacy; new weapons are invented and deployed. The power of the human brain can be unleashed with the massive potential for integration with computers and for cures for the ill and disabled. Still, the question must be asked: if we could all effectively collaborate, creating innovation ecosystems that share and invent the extraordinary daily, curing the disabled and elderly, how would we all survive? Space junk is a serious human-made obstacle to our ability to flee the Earth should war and environmental devastation make it uninhabitable. But these will only be a select few explorers sent off into the next frontier. What about the rest of us?

Sustainability is essential, and some of the most important leaps in sustainable living and development are happening in one of the most inhospitable regions in the world. The Middle East is embarking on an entirely new future, one led by leaders who have learned from others' past mistakes and are rapidly investing in projects that will benefit all of humanity. I am incredibly proud to be part of these endeavors, as every trip to the Middle East allows me to see hundreds of acres of new solar arrays, efficient buildings rising from what was once desert, each using recyclable materials that enable entire populations to embrace a brighter, smarter future. What I see is the product of decades of failures and lessons learned.

Once only dreamed of, the future is now. We can no longer be mere witnesses, but must take responsibility and guide it, own it. We have run dry of excuses, and our imaginations have never been freer.

I've talked to Israelis who were there when their long-dreamed nation finally became a reality. How they struggled against all odds, dug ditches, and served until their country was thriving. Imagine the pride!

Or think of my friend Viktor in Moscow, who witnessed the glories of the USSR and speaks glowingly of when the Soviets were leading the race into space, communism competing toe-to-toe with American capitalism. Then watch as his eyes lower when the subject of today's Russia is mentioned.

What was it like in 1976 to be in the garage when Steve Wozniak and Steve Jobs first invented the Apple computer? Or at the Indian Space Research Organization's headquarters on August 20, 2023, when its module safely landed on the moon! These are the moments we want to witness. And they're the product of countless hours of dedicated work by innovators who wanted to do something extraordinary.

There will be more of these moments coming soon. Innovation ecosystems remain hard at work, whether in secret or announced to the public by governments and companies, lost amid our overwhelming mix of news and social media. These are dynamic creations, ever evolving and expanding as new innovation ecosystems are being developed and deployed regularly, spreading collaboration and the need for newer, better products and services for all of humanity. World peace and prosperity seem like almost quaint concepts these days, yet they must remain our goals.

Tens of millions of Ukrainians and Russians would like nothing more than a single day without bombings, suspicious drones, or too many foreign interests involved in their lives. The invaluable people who make Taiwan's priceless silicon wafers are hard at work, forced to ignore the growing navy fleets and war games played by superpowers surrounding their small island nation. The descendants of Bedouins in Saudi Arabia now surveying the location for NEOM's new buildings, sustainably designed and solar powered, soon welcoming brilliant minds from afar to take the next great leap.

The need is urgent and the solutions are at our fingertips. My genes may turn against me, giving me the same brain cancer that claimed my father. Right now, DeepMind computers are studying my inherited riddle, millions of molecules processed per second to find that single flaw in my design, hopefully leading to a cure.

As a world community, we can no longer say that we don't have the means or ability to save ourselves. Do we have the will?

Innovate or die. Revive the corpse, or become one.

BIBLIOGRAPHY

Al-Sibai, Noor. "It Turns Out SpaceX and Tesla Get Way More Government Money Than NPR." *Futurism.com*, April 15, 2023. https://futurism.com/the-byte/spacex-tesla-government-money-npr.

Associated Press. "China Expands Defense Budget 7.2 Percent, Marking Slight Increase." *AP News*, March 4, 2023. https://apnews.com/article/china-defense-budget-aircraft-carriers-cdac45c8d36a47cffda68be99b7c9ee7.

Bond, Shannon. "Meta Says Chinese, Russian Influence Operations Are among the Biggest It's Taken Down." *NPR*, August 29, 2023. https://www.npr

.org/2023/08/29/1196117574/meta-says-chinese-russian-influence-operations-are-among-the-biggest-its-taken-d

Keane, Sean. "Elon Musk: Neuralink Brain Implant Will Improve 'Bandwidth' of Human Communication." *CNET*, September 29, 2020. https://www.cnet.com/science/elon-musk-neuralink-brain-implant-will-improve-bandwidth-of-human-communication/.

Kelly, Stephen. "How Close Are We to Building Real-Life Lightsabers?" *BBC Science Focus Magazine*, May 24, 2022. https://www.sciencefocus.com/future-technology/how-close-are-we-to-building-real-life-lightsabers.

Lal, Anil Kumar. "China's New Laser Space Weapons Alarms the US." *Times of India*, April 4, 2023. https://timesofindia.indiatimes.com/blogs/rakshakindia/chinas-new-laser-space-weapons-alarms-the-us/.

Peter G. Petersen Foundation. "US Defense Spending Compared to Other Countries." April 24, 2023. https://www.pgpf.org/chart-archive/0053_defense-comparison.

Prisco, Joanna. "This Nigerian Woman Transforms Tires into Recycled Furniture." *Global Citizen*, July 16, 2018. https://www.globalcitizen.org/en/content/nigerian-woman-recycled-tires-olabanke-banjo/.

Reuters. "Russia Doubles 2023 Defense Spending Plan as War Costs Soar." August 3, 2023. https://www.reuters.com/world/europe/russia-doubles-2023-defence-spending-plan-war-costs-soar-document-2023-08-04/.

Sample, Ian. "AI-Powered Drone Beats Human Champion Pilots." *The Guardian*, August 30, 2023. https://www.theguardian.com/technology/2023/aug/30/ai-powered-drone-beats-human-champion-pilots.

Appendix A: Global Innovation Index, 2023

Top three innovation economies by region.
* Top three in Sub-Saharan Africa excludes island economies. The top five within the region, including all economies, comprise Mauritius (1st), South Africa (2nd), Botswana (3rd), Cabo Verde (4th), and Senegal (5th).
† Top three in Northern Africa and Western Asia excludes island economies. The top four within the region, including all economies, comprise Israel (1st), Cyprus (2nd), United Arab Emirates (3rd), and Türkiye (4th). *Source*: World Intellectual Property Organization (WIPO), *Global Innovation Index 2023: Innovation in the Face of Uncertainty* (Geneva: WIPO, 2023). DOI:10.34667/tind.48220. Reproduced under Creative Commons Attribution 4.0 International.

High-income	Upper middle-income	Lower middle-income	Low-income
1. Switzerland	1. China	1. India	1. Rwanda
2. Sweden ↑	2. Malaysia ↑	2. Viet Nam	2. Madagascar
3. United States ↓	3. Bulgaria ↓	3. Ukraine ☆	3. Togo ☆

Top three innovation economies by income group. *Source*: World Intellectual Property Organization (WIPO), *Global Innovation Index 2023: Innovation in the Face of Uncertainty* (Geneva: WIPO, 2023). DOI:10.34667/tind.48220. Reproduced under Creative Commons Attribution 4.0 International.

For both figures, note that ☆ indicates a new entrant into the top three in 2023; ↑↓ indicates movement in ranking (up or down) within the top three, relative to 2022.

GLOBAL INNOVATION INDEX 2023 RANKINGS

GII rank	Economy	Score
1	Switzerland	67.6
2	Sweden	64.2
3	United States	63.5
4	United Kingdom	62.4
5	Singapore	61.5
6	Finland	61.2
7	Netherlands	60.4
8	Germany	58.8
9	Denmark	58.7
10	Republic of Korea (South Korea)	58.6
11	France	56.0
12	China	55.3
13	Japan	54.6
14	Israel	54.3
15	Canada	53.8
16	Estonia	53.4
17	Hong Kong, China	53.3
18	Austria	53.2
19	Norway	50.7
20	Iceland	50.7

GII rank	Economy	Score
21	Luxembourg	50.6
22	Ireland	50.4
23	Belgium	49.9
24	Australia	49.7
25	Malta	49.1
26	Italy	46.6
27	New Zealand	46.6
28	Cyprus	46.3
29	Spain	45.9
30	Portugal	44.9
31	Czech Republic	44.8
32	United Arab Emirates	43.2
33	Slovenia	42.2
34	Lithuania	42.0
35	Hungary	41.3
36	Malaysia	40.9
37	Latvia	39.7
38	Bulgaria	39.0
39	Türkiye	38.6
40	India	38.1
41	Poland	37.7
42	Greece	37.5
43	Thailand	37.1
44	Croatia	37.1
45	Slovakia	36.2
46	Viet Nam	36.0
47	Romania	34.7
48	Saudi Arabia	34.5
49	Brazil	33.6
50	Qatar	33.4
51	Russian Federation	33.3

GII rank	Economy	Score
52	Chile	33.3
53	Serbia	33.1
54	North Macedonia	33.0
55	Ukraine	32.8
56	Philippines	32.2
57	Mauritius	32.1
58	Mexico	31.0
59	South Africa	30.4
60	Republic of Moldova	30.3
61	Indonesia	30.3
62	Iran	30.1
63	Uruguay	30.0
64	Kuwait	29.9
65	Georgia	29.9
66	Colombia	29.4
67	Bahrain	29.1
68	Mongolia	28.8
69	Oman	28.4
70	Morocco	28.4
71	Jordan	28.2
72	Armenia	28.0
73	Argentina	28.0
74	Costa Rica	27.9
75	Montenegro	27.8
76	Peru	27.7
77	Bosnia and Herzegovina	27.1
78	Jamaica	27.1
79	Tunisia	26.9
80	Belarus	26.8
81	Kazakhstan	26.7
82	Uzbekistan	26.2

GII rank	Economy	Score
83	Albania	25.4
84	Panama	25.3
85	Botswana	24.6
86	Egypt	24.2
87	Brunei Darussalam	23.5
88	Pakistan	23.3
89	Azerbaijan	23.3
90	Sri Lanka	23.3
91	Cabo Verde	23.3
92	Lebanon	23.2
93	Senegal	22.5
94	Dominican Republic	22.4
95	El Salvador	21.8
96	Namibia	21.8
97	Bolivia	21.4
98	Paraguay	21.4
99	Ghana	21.3
100	Kenya	21.2
101	Cambodia	20.8
102	Trinidad and Tobago	20.7
103	Rwanda	20.6
104	Ecuador	20.5
105	Bangladesh	20.2
106	Kyrgyzstan	20.2
107	Madagascar	19.1
108	Nepal	18.8
109	Nigeria	18.4
110	Lao People's Democratic Republic	18.3
111	Tajikistan	18.3
112	Côte d'Ivoire	18.2
113	United Republic of Tanzania	17.4

GII rank	Economy	Score
114	Togo	16.9
115	Nicaragua	16.9
116	Honduras	16.7
117	Zimbabwe	16.5
118	Zambia	16.4
119	Algeria	16.1
120	Benin	16.0
121	Uganda	16.0
122	Guatemala	15.8
123	Cameroon	15.3
124	Burkina Faso	14.5
125	Ethiopia	14.3
126	Mozambique	13.6
127	Mauritania	13.5
128	Guinea	13.3
129	Mali	12.9
130	Burundi	12.5
131	Niger	12.4
132	Angola	10.3

Appendix B: Global Artificial Intelligence

THE GLOBAL AI INDEX

Country	Overall	Talent	Infrastructure	Operating Environment	Research	Development	Government Strategy	Commercial	Scale	Intensity
United States	1	1	1	28	1	1	8	1	1	5
China	2	20	2	3	2	2	3	2	2	21
Singapore	3	4	3	22	3	5	16	4	10	1
United Kingdom	4	5	24	40	5	8	10	5	4	10
Canada	5	6	23	8	7	11	5	7	7	7
South Korea	6	12	7	11	12	3	6	18	8	6
Israel	7	7	28	23	11	7	47	3	17	2
Germany	8	3	12	13	8	9	2	11	3	15
Switzerland	9	9	13	30	4	4	56	9	16	3
Finland	10	13	8	4	9	14	15	12	13	4
Netherlands	11	8	16	15	10	13	28	20	11	8
Japan	12	11	5	10	20	6	18	23	6	25
France	13	10	11	25	15	18	13	10	9	20
India	14	2	59	12	30	21	38	13	5	51
Australia	15	14	44	62	6	16	14	22	15	14

Appendix B

Country	Overall	Talent	Infrastructure	Operating Environment	Research	Development	Government Strategy	Commercial	Scale	Intensity
Denmark	16	19	15	1	18	19	21	17	18	11
Sweden	17	15	21	2	13	17	44	16	19	12
Luxembourg	18	31	6	14	19	22	31	14	33	9
Ireland	19	17	26	19	27	10	29	15	28	13
Austria	20	25	34	5	16	23	33	27	22	18
Spain	21	18	18	16	24	26	4	32	12	28
Belgium	22	26	43	24	14	25	36	25	23	19
Italy	23	22	35	6	21	28	9	35	14	33
Norway	24	24	22	29	22	20	39	21	30	16
Estonia	25	34	33	17	35	29	19	8	38	17
Taiwan	26	30	9	52	26	12	42	33	25	24
Poland	27	16	31	20	33	32	11	43	21	34
UAE	28	48	4	42	34	39	24	29	29	31
Portugal	29	38	36	9	31	33	26	24	31	27
Russia	30	28	19	33	39	24	7	52	20	42
Saudi Arabia	31	53	20	18	37	41	1	26	26	36
Hong Kong	32	52	10	35	40	50	51	6	27	30
Malta	33	46	37	21	43	15	25	34	48	23
Czech Republic	34	37	46	34	32	30	17	41	35	32
Brazil	35	21	42	44	36	36	30	39	24	44
New Zealand	36	32	32	46	25	27	49	31	43	26
Slovenia	37	58	29	38	28	31	22	42	42	29
Hungary	38	42	30	27	38	40	35	38	37	38
Turkey	39	29	52	7	41	52	27	49	32	43
Iceland	40	50	41	45	23	38	54	19	52	22
Chile	41	51	14	50	50	47	20	30	34	40
Qatar	42	62	25	47	17	48	46	55	49	35
Lithuania	43	41	40	36	44	34	34	37	47	37
Malaysia	44	40	17	49	42	44	43	45	40	41

Country	Overall	Talent	Infrastructure	Operating Environment	Research	Development	Government Strategy	Commercial	Scale	Intensity
Greece	45	27	51	58	29	37	52	40	51	39
Indonesia	46	23	57	37	48	55	40	44	36	52
Vietnam	47	36	38	57	54	43	32	51	39	49
Colombia	48	47	49	54	57	45	12	56	41	48
Argentina	49	45	48	32	55	51	37	57	46	50
Slovakia	50	54	45	26	53	46	45	50	50	45
Mexico	51	39	53	41	46	49	41	60	45	54
Egypt	52	43	55	55	45	56	23	53	44	55
Uruguay	53	55	27	39	61	42	48	48	54	47
Armenia	54	35	50	51	59	35	61	46	56	46
South Africa	55	57	56	31	51	54	61	28	53	57
Tunisia	56	44	54	53	47	53	58	61	57	53
Morocco	57	60	47	48	56	58	50	62	55	58
Bahrain	58	61	39	43	58	60	61	36	58	56
Pakistan	59	33	61	61	49	57	55	58	59	61
Sri Lanka	60	56	58	60	62	62	58	54	60	59
Nigeria	61	49	62	56	52	59	54	59	61	60
Kenya	62	59	60	59	60	61	56	47	62	62

Source: The Global AI Index, https://www.tortoisemedia.com/intelligence/global-ai/.

Appendix C: Global Trends, 2040

EMERGING DYNAMICS

International: More Contested, Uncertain, and Conflict-Prone. Key Takeaways:

- During the next two decades, power in the international system will evolve to include a broader set of sources and features with expanding technological, network, and information power complementing more traditional military, economic, and cultural soft power. No single state is likely to be positioned to dominate across all regions or domains, opening the door for a broader range of actors to advance their interests.
- The United States and China will have the greatest influence on global dynamics, supporting competing visions of the international system and governance that reflect their core interests and ideologies. This rivalry will affect most domains, straining and, in some cases, reshaping existing alliances, international organizations, and the norms and rules that have underpinned the international order.
- In this more competitive global environment, the risk of interstate conflict is likely to rise because of advances in technology and an expanding range of targets, new frontiers for conflict and a greater variety of actors, more difficult deterrence, and a weakening or a lack of treaties and norms on acceptable use.

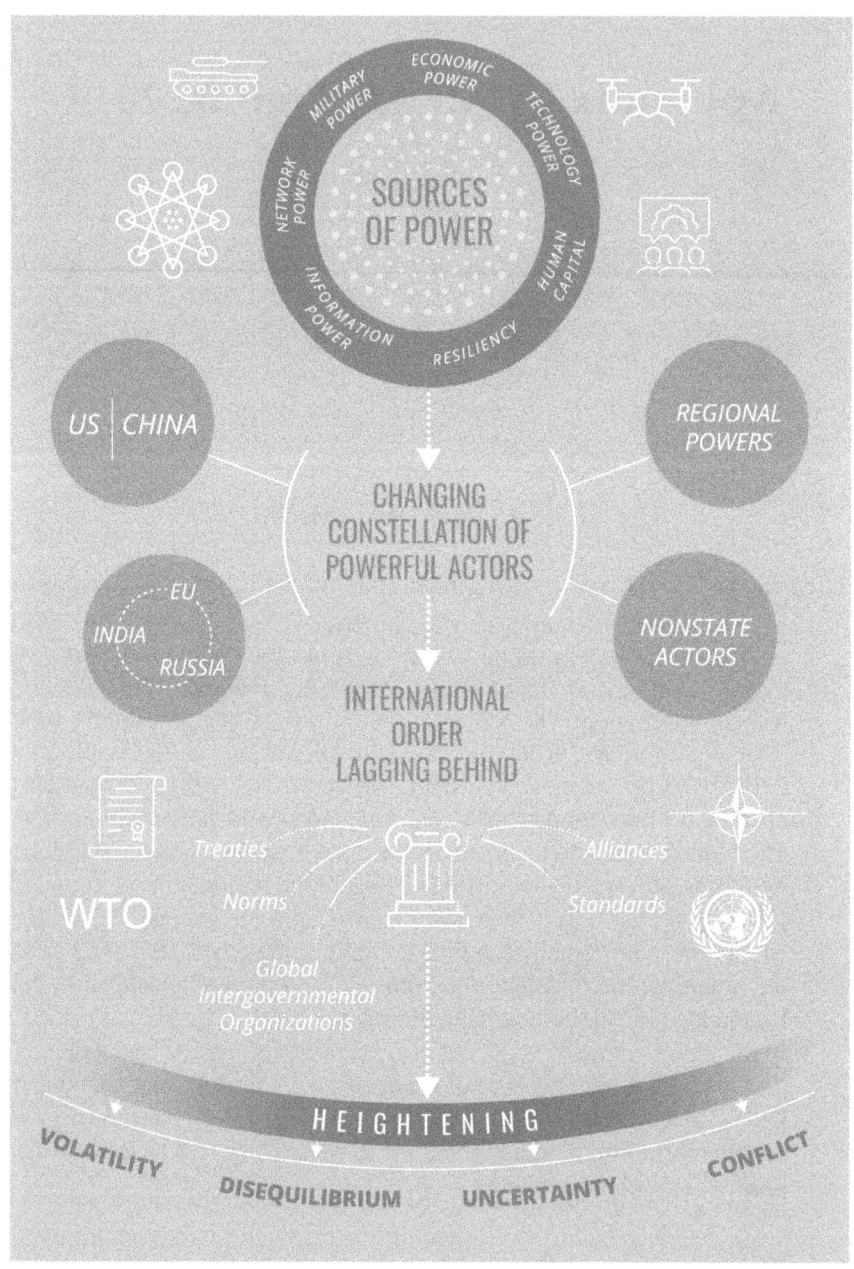

International dynamics. *Source*: National Intelligence Council, "Emerging Dynamics: International: More Contested, Uncertain, and Conflict Prone." *Global Trends 2040*, March 2021. https://www.dni.gov/index.php/gt2040-home/emerging-dynamics/international-dynamics.

Index

Abdullah of Jordan (King), 6
Adidas, 18
Afghanistan, xi, 11, 94, 103
Africa, ix, xii, 18, 47–48, 67–68, 100; health care, 59, 62, 63–64; oil and, 60–62, 64–66. *See also* Ethiopia; Nigeria; South Africa
African National Congress (ANC), 64
African Union, 61
aging, ix, 75
agriculture, 28, 35, 60–62, 63, 66–67
Ahmed, Abiy, 63
AI. *See* artificial intelligence
air defense systems, 9, 11, 29, 46
Air Force, US, 20
airforces, military, 7, 8
Alien (film), 107–8
Alphabet, 88
Alzheimer's disease, 74–75, 79, 87, 88
Amazon, vii, 9, 57
ANC. *See* African National Congress
Annual Climate Innovations Exchange (CLIX) summit, 97
Anti Money Laundering AI, 88
anti-Semitism, 11
Apple Inc., 18, 78, 112
Argentina, 95, 100
Arizona, TSMC with, 17, 21–22
arms (armaments), 9, 11, 49, 84, 89, 106; missiles, 19, 30–32, 46–48, 87, 96; sales, 30, 33, 47–48, 54, 55
artificial intelligence (AI), 29, 35, 49, 66, 68, 81, 83; ethics with standards for, x, 84–85, 87–90, 105; Global Artificial Intelligence Index, 121–23; quantum computing and, ix, x, 74, 75, 89; tools, 21, 67, 84–90, 105–6, 109, 112
Asian Football Cup (2023), 96
al-Assad, Bashar, 55
Atlantic Council, 56
atomic bomb test, USSR, 26
AT&T, 44
authoritarianism, ix, 19, 27–29, 31, 35, 57
autism spectrum disorder, 10
autocracies, 43, 97
Axle Infinity (online game), 46

Baltic states, 27
Bangladesh, 45–46, 89
Banjo, Olabanke, 108
banking, 46, 65, 88–90
basic research innovation, x, 30, 65, 83, 109; India, 76; Iran, 54, 56; Israel, 3, 7, 12; South Africa, 64, 66; Taiwan, 16

bazookas, antitank, 32
beer, 65–66
Beer Sheba, Israel, 9
Belt and Road Initiative, China, 18–19, 61, 79
Berkshire Hathaway, 21
Bhadla Solar Park, India, 76
bicycles, electronic, 32
Biden, Joe, 21, 32, 89
Bill and Melinda Gates Foundation, 63
biological weapons, 87, 89, 106
birth rates, 9, 27, 54, 63, 75
Bitcoin, 46, 104
Boeing Corporation, 9, 30
Bonocle, Qatar, 95
"Braille cell," 95
brain: drain with talent, 61, 64, 65, 66, 106; human, xii, 59, 74–75, 86–89, 90, 106, 111–12
Brazil, 44, 100
Brazil, Russia, India, China and South Africa bloc. *See* BRICS bloc
"breadbaskets," 28, 35, 66
breakthrough innovation, x, 56, 65, 83, 109; Israel, 3, 12; South Africa, 64; Taiwan, 16; US, 89
Brexit, ix, 76
bribery, 10, 48, 49, 64
BRICS (Brazil, Russia, India, China and South Africa) bloc, 100
Buffett, Warren, 21
Bushnell, David, 32

Canada, 15, 76, 103
cancer, xii, 73–76, 79, 112
Cancer Moonshot initiative, 74–76
carbon dioxide, 76, 77, 97, 99
Castel, Kevin, 85
censorship, 84, 85
Census Bureau, US, 61
ChatGPT, 21, 84–86
chemical weapons, 87, 106
chemistry databases, 87
children, 42, 63, 105

China, viii, 9, 27, 54, 60–61, 65, 84, 100, 103, 110–11; COVID-19 pandemic and, 18, 80, 96; economy, 18, 19, 22, 30, 35, 78; hackers, 45, 79; military, ix, 19, 22, 30, 47, 73; as peace broker, 34–35, 56, 77, 98, 99; relations with, 16–18, 20–21, 33, 35, 41, 43–45, 47–48, 56, 62–63, 67, 77–78, 89, 125
chips. *See* microchips
CHIPS and Science Act, US, 17
Churchill, Winston, viii, ix
Cisco, 9
classified intelligence systems, 17
climate, 10, 76, 97, 99
CLIX summit. *See* Annual Climate Innovations Exchange summit
Cold War, 7, 19, 32, 35, 96
communications, 11, 65, 73, 78, 85; monitoring of, 54, 79; telecommunications, 27, 44, 61–63, 67, 110
Congress, US, ix
conscription, military, 5, 6, 7, 8, 9
Cooperative Cyber Defence Centre of Excellence, NATO, 78–79
corporations, x, xi, 6, 33–34, 68, 79, 105
corruption, ix, 8, 10, 30–31, 35, 48–49, 59–60, 64–65
COVID-19 pandemic, xii, 18, 30, 48, 79–80, 96, 99
crime, xi, 7, 45–46, 49–50, 55, 74, 79
Crimea, 29–31
crypto, 34, 46, 104
cryptography system, quantum, 46
currency, 6, 17, 34, 46, 48, 104
"curse of crude," 60
customer service, AI and, 90
cyberattacks, 79, 80, 89
cybercrime, 79
cybertechnology, 9
cybertheft, 50
cyberthreat, 10, 79

cyberweapons, 55, 89
Cyrus45 Factory, Nigeria, 108

DARPA (Defense Advanced Research Project Agency), 29
data, vii, x, 10–11, 20, 87, 99, 110–11; Evans Data Corporation study, 89; sets and AI, 85–86
deaths, xii, 42–43, 48, 63, 74–75, 109
DeepMind, Google, 86–87, 89, 112
Defense Advanced Research Project Agency. *See* DARPA
Dell, 9
demilitarized zone (DMZ), 46, 49
democracy, 15, 16, 28
"Demokratizatsiya," 27
denial of service (DNS) attacks, 34
Denmark, 75
Department of Defense, US, xi
digital ambassadors, diplomacy with, x, 34, 78
digital infrastructure, 18–19, 61–62, 65, 67, 77–80, 95–96, 98
Digital Silk Road, China, 18–19, 61, 62, 65, 67, 77, 79
digitization, x, 34, 104
diplomacy, x, 6, 20, 34–35, 57, 78, 111
"directed energy" weapons, 29
disabled population, 95, 111
disinformation, 34, 111
disruptive innovation, x, 65, 83, 109; India, 76; Iran, 56; Israel, 3, 7, 8, 12; North Korea, 48; Russia, 29; South Africa, 63, 66; Taiwan, 16
disruptive technology, 12, 83
DMZ. *See* demilitarized zone
DNA, 73–75, 87
DNS attacks. *See* denial of service attacks
Dongguan YueYuen shoe factory, China, 18
drones, 5, 8–11, 31–34, 53, 55, 90, 108–9
drugs, xi, 48, 75, 87

Eagle, HMS, 32
economy: finances, 6, 17, 27–28, 32, 34, 45–46, 48, 65, 88–90, 104–5; fintech, 104–5; GDP, 12, 18, 29, 47, 61–62, 64, 76, 78, 97, 105; global, 12, 18–19, 22, 27–30, 35, 44, 47, 53–54, 62, 67, 76–78, 96–97, 99, 104–5
Edison, Thomas, 81
education, xii, 17, 45, 49, 78, 89; Africa and, ix, 59, 61, 62, 67; Middle East, 9, 10, 54, 96, 99
Education City Stadium, Qatar, 96
Egypt, 4–8, 11, 48, 100
Einstein, Albert, 88
Elbit, Israel, 8
Eldagsen, Boris, 86
elderly population, 75, 111
elections, 27, 28, 29, 57, 64, 90, 110
emigration, 27, 35, 43, 49, 61, 64
emotional attachment, social media, 111
employment, 22, 27, 28, 54, 65, 66, 99
energy, xi, 30, 32, 56, 81, 94, 99; "directed energy" weapons, 29; solar, 66, 76–77, 97, 111. *See also* gas; oil
entertainment, 46, 86, 95
entrepreneurs, 63, 64, 65, 95
Eritrea, 63
espionage. *See* spying
Estonia, 78, 79
ethics, x, 84–85, 87–90, 104–5
Ethiopia, 60, 62–63, 65, 67
EU. *See* European Union
Europe, 60, 77, 103; energy, xi, 30, 32; relations with, 18, 28, 31, 35
European Union (EU), ix, xi, 27, 34, 56, 87, 111; Horizon Europe, 76; Ukraine and, 28, 29, 32
Evans Data Corporation study (2017), 89

FDA. *See* Food and Drug Administration
Federal Bureau of Investigation, 79
fighter jets, 7, 8, 20

finances, 32, 45, 105; banking, 27–28, 46, 65, 88–90; currency, 6, 17, 34, 46, 48, 104
fintech (financial tech), 104–5
First Arab–Israeli War (1948), 4, 5–6, 11
Fisher, Paul, 26
Food and Drug Administration (FDA), US, 87
Forbes 20 high-net-worth individuals, xi
Foreign Affairs (magazine), 61
Fortune 500 companies, 9
Foxconn, Taiwan, 18, 78
FPI. *See* Russian Foundation for Advanced Research Projects
France, viii, ix, 7, 8, 30, 56, 93, 95
franchises, China with, 19, 79
frugal innovation, x, 65, 83, 109; Hamas, 11; Iran, 54–57; Israel, 3, 4–5, 7, 8, 11, 12; North Korea, 41, 44, 48, 49, 55, 57; South Africa, 64; Ukraine, 28, 31
FTX, 104

Gaddafi, Muammar, 35, 57
Gallup poll (2023), 59
gangs, xi, 61
Gartner Research, 84
gas: natural, xi, 28, 29, 30, 32, 77, 96; VX nerve, 87, 89
Gates, Bill, 63
GDP. *See* gross domestic product
General Electric, 8, 16
"genius" visas, 9
Georgia, 27, 30
Germany, ix, 6, 25, 32, 75, 78, 103
glial cells, brain, 88
Global Artificial Intelligence Index, 121–23
Global Initiative Against Transnational Organized Crime, 55
Global Innovation Index 2023, 60, 99; leaders, 115–16; rankings, 116–20
global positioning system (GPS), 29, 83, 108, 110
Global Trends 2040, 125–26
"golden" passports, 103, 104
Google, vii, 9, 61, 86–89, 99, 112
Gorbachev, Mikhail, 27
GPS. *See* global positioning system
GPU. *See* graphics processing unit
graft, corruption, 30–31, 35, 65
graphics processing unit (GPU), 21
Great Britain, viii, ix, 4–7, 32, 86, 93, 103
Great Plains, US, 35
gross domestic product (GDP): Apple and, 78; worldwide, 12, 18, 29, 47, 61–62, 64, 76, 78, 97, 105
Group of Seven, Moscow, 27
Guardians of Peace, North Korea, 45
The Guardian (newspaper), 95
guerrilla warfare, ix, 8, 42
Gulf Organization for Research and Development, 95

hackers, x, 34, 45–48, 79, 89, 90
"hallucinations," AI, 85, 87
Hamad Bin Khalifa University, Qatar, 95
Hamas, 8, 11, 53, 105
Hannibal of Carthage, xi, 89, 108
"happiness deficit," 59
Harvey, Thomas, 88
Health Affairs (website), 75
health care, viii, 9, 48–49, 59, 62, 64, 80; cancer, xii, 73–76, 79, 112; innovation, 63, 73, 74. *See also* COVID-19 pandemic
heart transplant, 63–64
Hebrew teachings, ancient, 60
Henley & Partners, 103
Hermes and Heron drone systems, 8
Hezbollah, 8
Hitler, Adolf, viii, ix, 25
Holocaust, reparations for, 6
Homo naledi, 59
Horizon (2020) Europe, 76
House of Saud, 98, 99
HSBC, 46, 88–89

Huang, Jensen, 21
Huawei, China, 19, 61
hubris, 81, 108
Human Genome Project, 73, 74, 87
Hussein, Saddam, 35, 55
hybrid ecosystem, Israel, 6, 8, 9
hypersonic missiles, 30–31, 46–47

IBM, 9
ICBMs. *See* intercontinental ballistic missiles
IDF. *See* Israel Defense Forces
immigration, 5–7, 9, 41, 45, 61, 64–66, 98, 106
India, ix, 27, 33, 76, 78, 100, 112
Indian Space Research Organization, 112
Industrial Technology Research Institute (ITRI), 17
information technology (IT), ix, 45, 76, 105
information warfare, 34, 111
infrastructure: digital, 18–19, 61–62, 65, 67, 77–80, 95–96, 98; projects, ix, 6, 18–19, 61, 62, 63, 66, 79, 97
innovation: accelerators and centers, 54; as entertainment, 95; Global Innovation Index 2023, 60, 99, 115–20; health care, 63, 73, 74; military, 10, 30, 32, 35, 73, 74; shared, 56, 76; subpar, 31, 42; UAE National Strategy for Advanced Innovation, 97
innovation strategies, vii, 17, 21–22. *See also* basic research innovation; breakthrough innovation; disruptive innovation; frugal innovation; sustaining innovation
intelligence, 4, 10–11, 17, 32–34, 46, 80
intercontinental ballistic missiles (ICBMs), 19, 46, 47, 48
international aid, 62, 63, 64, 65
International Atomic Energy Agency, 56
International Business Report (2016), 63

internet, 9, 29, 44–45, 60–62, 78, 84–85, 95
The Interview (film), 45
inventors, 81, 95, 97, 99, 105
iPhones, 78
Iran, 35, 55, 80, 100, 105; innovation strategies, 54–57; relations with, 33, 47, 48, 53, 56–58, 77, 96, 98
Iraq, xi, 4, 5, 11, 53, 55, 96
IRGC. *See* Islamic Revolutionary Guard Corps
Iron Dome air defense system, Israel, 9, 11, 46
Islamic Republic Army, 57
Islamic Revolutionary Guard Corps (IRGC), 54
Israel, 10, 33, 41, 46, 61, 105, 109; with hybrid ecosystem, 6, 8, 9; innovation strategies, 3, 4–5, 7, 8, 11, 12; relations with, 4, 6–8, 11, 55, 57, 77, 98–99
Israel Aerospace Industries, 8
Israel Defense Forces (IDF, "Tzahal"), 4, 8, 10
IT. *See* information technology
Italy, xi, 79, 103, 107, 108
ITRI. *See* Industrial Technology Research Institute

Japan, 32, 42, 47, 48, 77, 78
JCPOA. *See* Joint Comprehensive Plan of Action
Jenner, Edward, 73
Jobs, Steve, 112
Joint Comprehensive Plan of Action (JCPOA), 55–56
Jonathan, Goodluck, 60
Jordan, 4, 5, 6, 7–8, 11

Kakhovka Dam, bombing of, 31–32
kickbacks, corruption, ix, 30, 64
Kim Il-Sung, 41, 42–43, 49
Kim Jong-Il (son), 41, 44, 46
Kim Jong-Un (grandson), 33, 41–42, 45–50, 80

Kim Ju Ae (great-granddaughter), 49
Kim Yo-Jong (granddaughter), 48–49
King Abdullah University of Science and Technology, Saudi Arabia, 99
"knowledge-based" economy, 53, 54
Korean Armistice Agreement (1953), 41
Korean War, 41, 43
Kushner, Jared, 96–97

Lady R (ship), 64
land, UN-mandated, 4, 12
languages, 25, 93, 95
Lawrence "of Arabia," T. E., 93, 100
Lazarus Group, North Korea, 45
leaders, Global Innovation Index 2023, 115–16
Libya, xii, 57, 60
life expectancies, 27
Lockheed Martin, 20, 30

Mandela, Nelson, 64
Manhattan Project, US, 25
manufacturing, 8, 16–18, 21–22, 45, 66; military, 4, 19, 27, 33, 34; pharmaceutical, 28
Marshall Plan, 77
medicine. *See* health care; pharmaceuticals
megacorporations, 6, 34
metallurgy, 28, 35
microchips (chips), 16, 17, 21–22, 74, 84, 106
Microsoft, 9, 45, 55, 84, 89, 99
Middle East, viii–ix, 6, 9–10, 12, 93, 106, 111; digital infrastructure, 95–96, 98; Iraq, xi, 4, 5, 11, 53, 55, 96; Libya, xii, 57, 60; oil and, 33, 53, 54, 60, 77, 80, 94, 97–100. *See also* Iran; Israel; Qatar; Saudi Arabia; United Arab Emirates
migration, 16–17, 77, 98. *See also* emigration; immigration
military, viii, xi, 15, 42, 54, 57, 74, 77, 106; China, ix, 19, 22, 30, 47, 73; drones, 5, 8–11, 31–34, 53, 55, 109;

Israel, 3–11, 46; NATO, ix, 12, 56, 78–80, 87; North Korea, 43, 46–48, 55; Russia, 19–20, 29–35, 47, 49, 53, 64, 84; Ukraine, 29, 31–32, 33, 34; US, 8, 16, 19–22, 25, 27, 30, 33, 43, 46–47, 55, 78, 94, 110; USSR, 27. *See also* arms
mining, 27, 33, 53
missiles, 19, 30–32, 46–48, 87, 96
Mobility Innovations Center, Qatar, 95
Mohammed bin Rashid Al Maktoum Solar Park, 97
Mohammed bin Salman (Crown Prince of Saudi Arabia), 98, 99
molecules, toxic, 87, 89
moonshot programs, 7, 73, 74–76
Musk, Elon, 30, 74, 85, 90
Muslims, 77, 93–94, 96
Mutter Medical Museum, Philadelphia, 88

National Aeronautics and Space Administration (NASA), 26, 76, 96, 110
National Institute of Standards and Technology, US, 89
national security, 8, 17, 21
National Strategy for Advanced Innovation (2018), UAE, 97
National Vision 2030 (Qatar), 96, 99
nation-states, ix, x, 33–34, 68, 78–79, 105
NATO. *See* North Atlantic Treaty Organization
natural resources, 4, 10, 54, 59, 65, 94
navies, military, ix, 19, 29, 32, 64, 112
Navy, US, 55
NEOM initiative, Saudi Arabia, 10, 77, 98, 99, 100, 112
nerve gas, VX, 87, 89
Netanyahu, Benjamin, 10, 11
Neuralink brain implant, 74
neurotechnology, 74, 106
New Arab Cold War, 96
New Balance, 18

Nigeria, 60–63, 65–67, 106, 108
Nike, 18
North Atlantic Treaty Organization (NATO), ix, 12, 56, 78–80, 87
North Korea, viii, 35, 50, 79–80, 105, 109; innovation strategies, 41, 44, 48, 49, 55, 57; relations with, 33, 41–49, 53, 56, 89; with subpar innovation, 42
nuclear power, 57, 97
nuclear programs, 10, 47, 48, 55–57
Nvidia Corporation, 21, 84

Obama, Barack, 29
O'Brien, Robert, 21
oil, xi, 6, 7, 27, 76; Africa and, 60–62, 64–66; Middle East and, 33, 53, 54, 60, 77, 80, 94, 97–100; Russia and, 30, 32–33, 35, 54, 77, 80, 84, 98
oligarchs, ix, 27–31, 33
OPEC (Organization of Petroleum Exporting Countries), 98, 99
Orange Revolution, Ukraine, 28
Organization of Petroleum Exporting Countries. *See* OPEC
Ottoman Empire, 93
outsourcing, 16–18, 21, 76

Pakistan, 81, 108
Palestinian Liberation Organization (PLO), 8
Palestinians, 4, 6, 8, 10, 11
Pamaz Agreement (1950s), 6
Park, Yeonmi, 43–44
Parkinson's disease, 74, 75, 88, 106
passports, 103–4
peace, 34–35, 45, 56, 77, 94, 96, 98–99, 112
pens and pencils, in space, 26
pharmaceuticals, 28, 48, 60, 66, 75, 87, 90
phones, cell, 11, 65, 78, 85
PLO. *See* Palestinian Liberation Organization
"police stations," China, 34

polio eradication, 63
politics, AI and, 85
populations, 29, 60, 95, 96; birth rates, 9, 27, 54, 63, 75; elderly, 75, 111
pornography, 84–85
Prigozhin, Yevgeny, 33
Prince Mohammed bin Salman bin Abdulaziz University for Digital Science and Technology, Saudi Arabia, 99
prison camps, 42, 49
"proof of concept," 104
propaganda, 32, 41–43, 45, 80, 85, 110–11
protests, 10, 18, 22, 54, 57, 80, 86
"Pseudomnesia," 86
Putin, Vladimir, 28–33, 35, 49, 80, 83, 84

al-Qaeda, 105
QASA. *See* Qatar Aeronautics and Space Agency
Qatar, 94–97, 99–100
Qatar Aeronautics and Space Agency (QASA), 96
Qatar Science & Technology Park, 95
quantum computing, ix, x, 46, 74, 75, 80, 89, 106
"quantum processor," 57

Radio Corporation of America (RCA), 16–17
Ramaphosa, Cyril, 64
rankings, Global Innovation Index 2023, 116–20
RCA. *See* Radio Corporation of America
R&D. *See* research and development
RDT&E. *See* research, development, test, and evaluation
Reagan, Ronald, 27
Reebok, 18
refugees, 4, 6, 11, 12, 47, 110
reinforcement learning (RL), AI, 49, 86–87, 89

research, 17, 29–30, 84, 95, 112. *See also* basic research innovation
research, development, test and evaluation (RDT&E), 21
research and development (R&D), 9, 78, 95, 99, 106; Africa, 61, 64, 65; Russia, ix, 29–31, 35
Rising Star cave system, South Africa, 59
RL, AI. *See* reinforcement learning, AI
robotics, 29, 84, 90, 95, 107–8
rockets, 9, 11, 30, 46–49
Roman legions, xi, 3, 89
Russia, 27, 28, 41, 56, 79, 100, 105; with innovation, 29, 31; military, 19–20, 29–35, 47, 49, 53, 64, 84; oil and, 30, 32–33, 35, 54, 77, 80, 84, 98; in Ukraine, viii–ix, 19–20, 25, 29, 31–35, 49, 53, 55, 83–84, 94, 98–99, 104, 108, 112
Russian Foundation for Advanced Research Projects (FPI), 29–30, 84

sanctions, 33, 85; Iran with, 53, 54, 56, 57, 105; North Korea with, 41, 47, 48, 105; Russia with, 30, 34, 64, 84, 98, 105
sandboxes, 104–6
sanitation systems, 62, 66
satellites, 10, 26–27, 30, 47–48, 65, 96, 110
Saudi Arabia, 35, 56, 81, 94, 96–97; NEOM initiative, 10, 77, 98, 99, 100, 112; oil and, 33, 60, 77, 80, 98, 99
scams, 61–62
science and technology (S&T), 44, 45, 60, 65, 95, 99
Scotland Yard, xi
security, 8, 12, 17, 21, 34, 61
Security Council, UN, 78
self-interests, 5, 36
semiconductors, 16–17, 21–22, 83, 84
sentience, computers, 21, 84, 87
Shahed drone systems, 33, 55
sight-impaired population, 95

Silicon Valley, 65, 105; in Middle East, 9, 94, 100; in US, vii–viii, 78, 94, 99
Singapore: economy, 104–5; passports, 103–4
Six-Day War, 7–8
social media, vii, 19, 54, 85, 110–11, 112
soft power, 77–79, 125
software developers, 9, 45, 89–90
solar arrays, 66, 111
solar farms, 76–77
solar park, 76, 97
Somalia, 55
songbun caste system, 42, 43, 49
Sony Pictures, 45
Sony World Photography Award, 86
South Africa, 60, 62, 67, 100; immigration and, 64, 65, 66, 106; innovation strategies, 63, 64, 66; Rising Star cave system, 59
South America, 6, 18, 78, 100
Southeast Asia, 18, 100, 106
South Korea, 41, 43–44, 46–49, 78
South Pars/North Dome gas field, 96
space, 26, 30, 76, 83, 96, 110–12
Space Command, US, 110
Space Force, US, 110
SpaceX, 30
Spain, 44, 103
Spartans, 108
Spiez Laboratory, Switzerland, 87, 105–6
Sputnik 1, 26
Sputnik V (COVID-19 vaccine), 80
spying (espionage), 19, 34, 45, 47, 48, 67, 110
S&T. *See* science and technology
Stanford University, 86
Stars of Science (TV show), 95
Star Wars (film), 107
"Star Wars" air defense system, US, 46
State Armaments Program, Russia, 84
stolen technology, 33, 35, 46–47, 55, 56–57
Stuxnet virus, 55, 89

submarines, 32
submersible drones, 32, 34
Suez Canal, 7
"suicide" attack drones, 33
supply chains, 18, 21, 78
sustainable development, viii, 76, 96
sustaining innovation, x, 30, 56, 65, 66, 83; India, 76; Israel, 3, 12; UAE, 98
SwiftAI, 109
Switzerland, 60, 87, 105–6, 109
Sykes–Picot Agreement, 93
Syria, 4, 5, 6, 7, 11, 55

Taiwan, 15, 75, 78, 105; innovation strategies, 16; relations with, 16–18, 20–21, 47; with semiconductors, 16–17, 21–22
Taiwan Semiconductor Manufacturing Company (TSMC), 16, 17, 21–22
talent, vii, viii, 48, 62, 76, 77; attracting, 5–6, 9, 45, 64–66, 84, 98–99, 106; brain drain, 61, 64, 65, 66, 106
Team of Four, Moscow, 27
"techno-authoritarian," 19
technology, viii, 9, 17, 29, 89, 97, 104; disruptive, 12, 83; IT, ix, 45, 76, 105; military, 8, 10, 20, 33; neurotechnology, 74, 106; S&T, 44, 45, 60, 65, 95, 99; stolen, 33, 35, 46–47, 55, 56–57
Tech Park, UAE, 97
telecommunications, 27, 44, 61–63, 67, 110
terrorism, 33, 53–54, 89–90
Tesla, 85, 90
Tesla, Nikola, 81
Texas, 76–77, 99
theft, 45–46, 49, 50
Third Economic Plan, North Korea, 44
Tigray people, 63
tires, recycling, 108
tourism, 15, 95, 97, 100
trade, ix, 12, 56, 60, 73, 97; costs, 18, 19, 64; deals, 6, 35, 44, 47, 54, 78, 79; illegal, viii, 50, 105

transportation, 9, 27, 73
Trump, Donald, 49, 56
TSMC. *See* Taiwan Semiconductor Manufacturing Company
Turkey, 35
"Turtle" (submarine), Bushnell's, 32
2022 State of AI in Africa, 66
Twitter (X), 85, 111
"Tzahal." *See* Israel Defense Forces

UAE. *See* United Arab Emirates
UAVs. *See* "uncrewed aerial vehicles"
UFOs, 109
Ukraine: passports, 103; relations with, 25–32, 35; Russia in, viii–ix, 19–20, 25, 29, 31–35, 49, 53, 55, 83–84, 94, 98–99, 104, 108, 112
"uncrewed aerial vehicles" (UAVs), 33, 55
underwater vehicles, unmanned, 29
unemployment, 22, 28, 54. *See also* employment
UNESCO, 54
Union of Soviet Socialist Republics (USSR), 7, 19, 78, 111; collapse of, 25, 27, 28; relations with, 26, 42–43
Unit 9900, IDF, 10
United Arab Emirates (UAE), 94, 98, 100; on Global Innovation Index, 99; relations with, 96–97
United Kingdom (UK), 10, 12, 75, 76; passports, 103; relations with, 20, 32, 35, 56, 98
United Nations (UN), xii, 29, 44, 54, 62; with mandated land in Middle East, 4, 12; Security Council, 8
United Nations of AI, x, 105
United States (US), ix, xi, 12, 41, 60–61, 79, 88–89, 103; Arizona, 17, 21–22; Cancer Moonshot initiative, 74–76; FDA, 87; intelligence, 4, 11, 32; military, 8, 16, 19–22, 25, 27, 30, 33, 43, 46–47, 55, 78, 94, 110; NASA and, 26, 76, 96, 110; relations with, 4, 6–7, 11, 16–18, 20–21, 26,

31–32, 35, 43–44, 47, 49, 55–56, 77–78, 97–98, 125; Silicon Valley, vii–viii, 78, 94, 99; Texas, 76–77, 99
University of California, Berkeley, 86
University of Zurich, 109
uranium, 55–56
USAID, 62
USSR. *See* Union of Soviet Socialist Republics

vaccinations, 73, 79–80
Vietnam, 18, 78
violence, 61, 73, 84
virus, 55, 88, 89. *See also* COVID-19 pandemic
visas, 9, 103

Wagner Group, 33–34
Wall Street, vii, 84
water, 29, 32, 62, 84, 95, 97, 110; drinking, 44, 66, 81, 94, 108; shortages, 22, 100
Wells, H. G., 107
WGA. *See* Writers Guild of America

wind farms, 77
women, 5, 53, 108
World Bank, 27–28
World Cup, FIFA, 44, 94–96, 100
World Happiness Report (2022), 59
World Health Organization, xii, 48
World Intellectual Property Organization, 60
World War II, viii, xi, 4–7, 25, 43, 77, 81
Wozniak, Steve, 112
Writers Guild of America (WGA), 86

Yanukovych, Viktor, 28, 29
Yeltsin, Boris, 28
Yemen, 55

Zelenskyy, Volodymyr, ix, 32
Zhongxing Telecommunications Equipment (ZTE), 61
Zimbabwe, 60
ZTE. *See* Zhongxing Telecommunications Equipment
Zuma, Jacob, 64

About the Author

Edoardo Giglio is a seasoned professional at the intersection of technology and strategic risk, drawing from a distinguished career that spans continents and industries. A polymath with academic credentials from the University of London's School of Oriental and African Studies, City Law School, the London School of Economics and Political Science, the University of Cambridge, and the American Military University, Edoardo has mastered disciplines ranging from political science and international law to emerging technology, cyberstrategy, and space studies with a specialization in aerospace engineering. He is currently a doctoral candidate at the University of Reading researching the influence of technology innovation ecosystems on geopolitics from the Cold War to the Global War on Terrorism. Having worked in covert intelligence and as a High-Tech Crime/CID investigator with New Scotland Yard, Edoardo's expertise in cybersecurity, technology innovation strategies, and geopolitical threats informs his captivating narratives. His entrepreneurial journey, always at the forefront of technology and strategic risk, has led him to advise Forbes20 HNWI, philanthropic organizations, multinationals, and international organizations. As the former head of a private risk advisory firm he founded, Edoardo's career has taken him to some of the world's most remote and challenging locations, from the African savannah to the deserts of the Middle East, imbuing his work with authenticity and vividness. Now an advisor to governments, Edoardo's thought-provoking perspective weaves together technology, innovation, and their profound effects on geopolitics.